WILLIAM H. WILLIMON's
LAST LAUGH

WILLIAM H. WILLIMON's

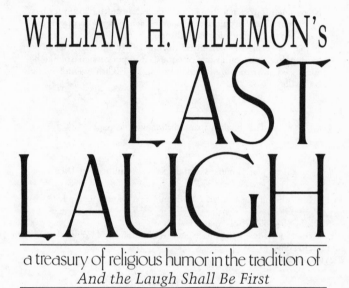

LAST LAUGH

a treasury of religious humor in the tradition of
And the Laugh Shall Be First

Compiled by
WILLIAM H.
WILLIMON

ABINGDON PRESS
Nashville

WILLIAM H. WILLIMON'S LAST LAUGH

Copyright © 1991 by Abingdon Press

This book is printed on acid-free paper.

Library of Congress Cataloging—in-Publication Data

William H. Willimon's last laugh / William H. Willimon, compiler.
  p.   cm.
  ISBN 0-687-45598-7 (alk. paper)
  1. Wit and humor—Religious aspects—Christianity. I. Willimon, William H.
BR115.H84W54   1991
202'.07—dc20   90-49556
                                                                      CIP

Scripture quotations are from the New Revised Standard Version Bible, Copyright © 1989, by the Division of Christian Education of the National Council of the Churches of Christ in the United States of America.

MANUFACTURED IN THE UNITED STATES OF AMERICA

Frederick Buechner recalls his conversion during a sermon by George Buttrick:

[George Buttrick] said that unlike Elizabeth's coronation in the Abbey, this coronation of Jesus in the believer's heart took place among confession—and I thought, yes, yes, confession—and tears he said—and I thought tears, yes, perfectly plausible that the coronation of Jesus in the believing heart should take place among confession and tears. And then with his head bobbing up and down so that his glasses glittered, he said in an old odd, sandy voice, the voice of an old nurse, that the coronation of Jesus took place among confession and tears and then, as God was and is my witness, great laughter, he said. Jesus is crowned among confession and tears and great laughter, and at the phrase great laughter, for reasons that I have never satisfactorily understood, the great wall of China crumbled and Atlantis rose up out of the sea, and on Madison Avenue at 73rd Street, tears leapt from my eyes as though I had been struck across the face.[1]

[1]Frederick Buechner, *The Alphabet of Grace* (New York: Seabury Press, 1970), pp.43-44.

CONTENTS

WILLIAM H. WILLIMON's

LAST
LAUGH

INTRODUCTION

Here is a book that need not have been published. This book will not put food on anyone's table (except mine). It will not make a significant contribution to world peace, nor will it help The United Methodist Church to attract more members. The material within this book will not advance the scholarly discussion of religion. Reference to this volume will never appear as a footnote in a religion graduate student's dissertation. It has no point.

Besides, there is already one volume of religious humor, *And The Laugh Shall Be First*, so why do we need another? This book is unnecessary.

That may be about the best justification for why this second volume of religious humor is so desperately needed.

People—particularly Christian, religious people—tend to be serious. After all, who is a religious person if not the one who gives serious attention to that which is utterly essential and absolutely necessary? To be religious is to be concerned, ultimately concerned. Too many people go about life utterly unconcerned about world peace, hungry people, impending ecological disaster, and the justice of God. Religious people are those who attend to the necessary.

Yet here is our problem with humor. Humor is unnecessary. Norman Cousins, in *The Anatomy of an Illness*, claims that he cured himself of a serious illness by watching old Groucho Marx movies, suggesting that humor has therapeutic value. But Groucho was a comic, not a doctor, and his movies were made for good laughs, not good health. Fun, by its very nature, is basically unnecessary. It doesn't put food on anyone's table (except for the tables of comedians), it doesn't have some noble, overriding purpose or goal. In fact, when we try to justify having fun on the basis of its alleged utility in delivering something other than fun, then fun is no longer all that much fun. It's just something we do in order to get something else, just another utilitarian program, a serious strategy, a means to an end. That's work, not fun. We Americans tend to be so utilitarian, judging all experiences, persons, and activities on the basis of what good they can do us, rather than relaxing and enjoying them for no more noble purpose other than that they are fun.

We aren't jogging for the fun of it; we are "working out." We aren't laughing for the sheer, pointless fun of it; we are improving our mental health. Where's the fun in that?

A Professor of Laughter might define humor as that type of auditory or visual stimulation that provokes the laughter reflex in the human being.

Immediately, we confront the central paradox of humor. Motor reflexes within the human body all have some adaptive or protective purpose. The pupil of the eye involuntarily contracts when it encounters bright light. The point of this contraction is obvious. When we touch a hot candle, we say, "Ouch" and automatically withdraw our hand from the heat.

But when we laugh, the movement of fifteen facial muscles, along with certain distinctive noises, occurs. The laughter reaction appears to have absolutely no utilitarian value, and contributes nothing to our struggle for survival. Among all the human reflexes, laughter is unique in that it has no apparent biological purpose.

One might call laughter a sort of luxury reflex. We can survive without it.

Animals appear not to laugh. Only humans laugh, or cry, though animal howling appears to come close to human crying. Not much that animals do comes close to our laughter. Perhaps that is because the so-called lower animals are still tied to the basics of animal survival. They are still engaged in the basic, carnal business of gathering food, producing and protecting their young, and eating or being eaten. It is only to humans that God—having so much extra creative time, or surplus biological equipment lying around by the sixth day of creation—gave the ability to laugh.

So perhaps that is why laughter, and the humor that evokes it, inherently tends toward excess. Satire, such as that found within this book, tends deliberately to overstate something. The victim's distinctive personality features are exaggerated. Foibles are magnified. Straight invective is not funny. Direct attack elicits only sympathy for the victim or hostility toward the perpetrator. To be funny, satire must deliberately overshoot its mark. It isn't funny if it isn't excessive.

Sometimes people say things about humor like, "I don't mind having a good time at someone else's expense, as long as our humor is not cruel," or, "Satire is fine, as long as it is done in kindness and not out of spite," or "Humor should never hurt."

Such sentiments are all well and good. In fact, they can even be said to be Christian in origin. However, they are unworkable. For one thing, when anyone has fun at my expense, puncturing my pride or assaulting my sacred cows, I tend to think it hurtful rather than humorous. How can the puncturing of pride feel otherwise? Never mind that their assault on my pride might just happen to be true. It still hurts.

For another thing, there is more than a touch of aggressiveness in nearly all humor—religious or otherwise. Someone has pointed out that in the Old Testament's twenty-nine references to laughter, no less than thirteen are directly linked to scorn, derision, mocking, and contempt. Only two are born of joy. I suppose the morality of such aggressive biblical laughter depends upon who is doing the laughing. The Psalmist says that "he who sits in the heavens laughs; the Lord has them in derision" (Ps. 2:4). Since God made us, God should certainly be able to laugh at us if God wants. Although, when the Creator laughs at the foibles of the creature, in a certain sense, the joke is also on the one who made us.

It is an eternal comfort for Psalm 2 to reassure us that God doesn't mind a good joke.

Aristotle was the first to note that laughter is usually tied to some form of aggressiveness. In humor, someone is being put down. When the oppressor is laughing with scorn over the sorry plight of the oppressed, it isn't funny. However, when the oppressed are thumbing their noses, in their laughter, at the oppressor, humor is getting very close to justice. So I say again: the morality of laughter depends upon who is doing the laughing.

The explosive laughter of a Sunday congregation when the preacher trips on his way out of the pulpit after a particularly pompous sermon is a measure of the congregation's aggressiveness, a release of emotion that reveals their pent-up resentment for liturgical boredom. Yet, even though their laughter may painfully puncture the preacher's pride, their laughter is less painful than dragging the preacher out of the pulpit and throwing him over a cliff, which is what one congregation tried to do to its preacher after a particularly tough sermon (Luke 4:16-30).

Karl Barth, in his mammoth *Church Dogmatics*, includes humor in his section on humility (III, 4, 662 ff.). Although I am not trying to defend humor that is ugly, hurtful, or derisive, I know of no way whereby I am made to face the humbling truth about myself, or to see myself as God sees me, or to begin to deal with my presumption and pride, without my being hurt in some manner. Although I will try to be big about humor at the expense of my pride, and may even muster a bit of a smile myself, I will still feel that I am being put down.

The old put down is involved in most all humor. Whether being put down is good or bad, at least from a Christian point of view, is not whether or not it hurts, but whether or not the one going down ought to go down.

Jesus promised that, in his kingdom, there would be a great

deal of role reversal going on, many going down who were once high and mighty. At his table, "all who exalt themselves will be humbled, and those who humble themselves will be exalted" (Luke 14:11).

But mostly what he promised was extravagance, a great deal of apparently useless, pointless grace. He told us so many stories of extravagant wine makers who generously paid those who worked only one hour in the vineyard as much as he paid those who had worked all day (Matt. 20:1-16); a father who gave his younger son his entire inheritance then, when his prodigal son returned after having blown all of his birthright in loose living, responded by throwing an exuberant party (Luke 15:11-32); a stranger who not only stopped to help a man in a ditch, but also risked everything for the man, bound up his wounds, and told the innkeeper that he would pay whatever bill the man accumulated during his recovery (Luke 10:25-37). And did you hear the one about the shepherd who left all ninety-nine sheep in the wilderness in order to go out and look for just one stray . . . ?

Evidently, when this God begins spreading around the grace, he doesn't exercise much caution. The precious seed of his word gets thrown all over the place, on good soil and bad, without much regard to where it lands (Mark 4:3-9). At the heart of the Good News, right at the center of it, is a God who throws caution to the winds and extravagantly, effusively, with a recklessness that can only be called comic, reaches out to us.

Two people went to church to pray. One person was a good, serious, ultimately concerned Pharisee like you or me, the other person was a no-good, cheating, immoral tax collector, such as those who would never buy a book such as this. You remember how the story ends. The good man, so full of it (full of his religion, that is) went back down to his house empty. That no-good tax collector got justified.

Once again, the joke is on us.

So many times, after Jesus told his perfectly outrageous stories of divine graciousness, his serious disciples wanted to know what was his point. Exasperated by anybody spoiling a perfectly funny joke by asking its point, Jesus could only say, "Let anyone with ears to hear listen!" (Mark 4:9).

To even ask the "point" is to reveal oneself to have missed the point.

One spring a reporter from our student newspaper called me and said, "Dr. Willimon, I am doing a story on things that are happening on campus at this time of year. Now over at the Chapel, what would you say is the goal of Easter?"

"The *goal* of Easter?" I asked.

"Yes," the reporter persisted. "What is its point, its purpose? Why do you do it?"

"Well we just do. Easter is just, well, it's just Easter. We just celebrate it."

I could see the headlines: DEAN OF CHAPEL SAYS EASTER IS POINTLESS.

From the utilitarian, pragmatic, serious—so deadly serious—perspective of modern people, much that we Christians do does seem pointless. Even Easter. We do it for no better purpose than the sheer fun of it.

That, modern people may one day discover, just may be the point after all.

> William H. Willimon
> Duke University Chapel
> April Fool's Day, 1990
> (Not on the church's calendar
> because, in a sense, every day
> is Fool's Day for the church.
> Read: Romans 1:18–2:5)

1

The authorship of this classic burlesque sermon has been in dispute for more than a hundred years. The sermon was delivered, according to tradition, by an old flatboat captain who was also a Hard-Shell Baptist preacher at Waterproof, Louisiana (then Mississippi), in the early 1850s. It soon appeared in newspapers all over the nation. It is the work of William Penn Brannan, an itinerant portrait painter and journalist from Cincinnati, who happened to be in the vicinity of Waterproof in the summer of 1851 and heard a sermon that inspired this piece of classic backwoods burlesque.

"THE HARP OF A THOUSAND STRINGS"*

William Penn Brannan

I may say to you, my brethering, that I am not an educated man, an I am not one o' them that beleeves education is necessary for a gospel minister, fur I beleeve the Lord educates his preachers jest as he wants em to be educated; and although I say it that oughtn't to say it, yet in the State of Indianny, whar I live, thar's no man as gits a bigger congregation nor what I gits.

"Thar may be some here today, my brethering, as don't know what persuasion I am uv. Well, I may say to you, my brethering, that I am a Hard Shell Baptist. Thar's some folks as don't like the Hard Shell Baptists, but I'd rather hev a hard shell as no shell at all. You see me here today, my brethering, dressed up in fine close; you mout think I was proud, but I am not proud, my brethering; and although I've been a preacher uv the gospel for twenty years and although I'm capting uv that flatboat that lies at your landing, I'm not proud, my brethering.

"I'm not gwine ter tell you *edzackly* whar my tex may be found; suffice it tu say, it's in the leds of the Bible, and you'll find it some whar 'tween the fust chapter of the book of Generation and the last chapter of the book of Revolutions, and if you'll go and sarch the Scriptures, you'll not only find my tex thar but a great many other texes will do you good to read; and my tex, when you shill find it, you shill find it to read thus:

And he played on a harp uv a thousand strings—sperits of just men made perfect.

"My tex, brethern, leads me to speak uv sperits. Now thar's a great many kind of sperits in the world. In the fust place, thar's the sperit as som folks call ghosts; then thar's the sperits uv turpen*time;* and then thar's the sperits as some folks call liquor, and I've got as good artikel uv them kind uv sperits on my flatboat as ever was fotched down the Mississippi River; but thar's a great many other kind of sperits, for the tex says: 'He played on a harp uv a thou-*sand* strings—sperits of just men made perfeck.'

"But I'll tell you the kind of sperits as is ment in the tex; it's fire. That is the kind of sperits as is ment in the tex, my brethering. Now thar's a great many kinds of fire in the world. In the fust place, thar's the common sort uv fire you light a segar or pipe with, and thar's camfire, fire before you're ready to fall back, and many other kinds uv fire, for the tex ses: 'He played on a harp uv a *thou*-sand strings—sperits uv just men made perfeck.'

"But I'll tell you the kind of fire as is ment in the tex, my brethering—it's *hell-fire!* an that's the kind of fire as a great many of you'll come to, ef you don't do better nor what you have bin doin—for 'He played on a harp uv a *thou*-sand strings—sperits of just men made perfeck.'

"Now, the different sorts uv fire in the world may be

likened unto the different persuasions in the world. In the first place, we have the 'Piscapalions, and they are a high salin and a highfalutin set, and they may be likened unto a turkey buzzard that flies up into the air, and he goes up and up till he looks no bigger than your fingernail, and the fust thing you know he cums down and down and is a-fillin himself on the karkiss of a dead hoss by the side uv the road—and 'He played on a harp of a *thou*-sand strings—sperits of just men made perfeck.'

"And then, thar's the Methodis, and they may be likened unto the squirrel runnin up into a tree, for the Methodis believes in gwine on from one degree uv grace to another and finally on to perfecshun; and the squirrel goes up and up, and he jumps from lim to lim, and branch to branch, and the fust thing you know, he falls, and down he comes kerflummux; and that's like the Methodis, for they is allers fallin from grace, ah! And 'He played on a harp of a *thou*-sand strings—sperits of just men made perfeck.'

"And then, my brethering, thar's the Baptist, ah! and they hev bin likened unto a possom on a 'simmon tree, and the thunders may roll, and then the earth may quake, but that possum clings there still, ah! And you shake one foot loose, and the other's thar; and you may shake all feet loose, and he laps his tail around the lim, and he clings furever—for 'He played on a harp of a *thou*-sand strings—sperits of just men made perfeck.'"

"FAREWELL, BROTHER CRAFFORD!"*

This story of Brannan's appeared in the Louisville Daily Courier, in March of 1856. The opening sentence refers to "The Harp of a Thousand Strings."

During my sojourn in Mississippi (shortly after I heard the great sermon which was played on a harp of a thousand strings), I had occasion to visit a friend in the neighborhood of Port Gibson. The next day being the Sabbath, I accompanied him to Zion Chapel. A new minister had been called to that neighborhood, and this was to be his salutatory sermon. Zion Chapel was some hundred yards from the main road and surrounded by forest trees. Having arrived rather too early for the service, my friend and I sauntered about the woods rather actively employed in brushing away the cloud of mosquitoes that surrounded us. At length a strange specimen of *genus homo* made his appearance on horseback; it was Brother Crafford.

His dress was decidely peculiar. On his head he wore an old-fashioned, bell-crown beaver several sizes too large. To remedy this defect, a cotton bandana handkerchief was stuffed between the hat and forehead. His coat was of a most ancient pattern—blue, with brass buttons, short waist, and long swallow-tail; the collar came within an inch of hiding the back part of his head. His vest was extremely long, and his pants ditto short. The latter were held down by a leather strap passed under a huge pair of brogans of an untanned leather color. Altogether, his presence strongly suggested Dan Marble in his Yankee character of Jonathan Homespun. But to the sermon—or at least a portion of it—for it was utterly impossible to report the whole.

*Reprinted by permission of Vanderbilt University Press, from *With the Bark On*, edited by John W. Anderson. Copyright © 1967.

The congregation was large as it had been "norated" abroad that a new minister was to make his debut at Zion. Brother Crafford slunk into the pulpit with more than ordinary humility, and after devoting a few moments to silent prayer he rose. Gingerly pushing up the sleeve of his *store coat*, he displayed a pair of large, long bony hands of a beet-red color; he grasped the handle of an earthen pitcher and poured into a tin cup a draught of water which he drank with inimitable gusto. His appearance in the pulpit was a study for an artist. His face was long and lank, eyes pale gray, nose aquiline, complexion sandy, hair grayish sandy, head bald on top with the exception of a small patch on the organ of reverence (as if to shade it). He began apologetically, as follows:

"You don't see me today in the dress I allers wear; I come among you as a stranger, and I am now tricked out in my store clothes; I am not a proud man, but I thought it would be more becoming before strangers." After this he raised a hymn in which the congregation joined. Then he began his sermon:

"My dear breethern and sisters, first and foremost, I'm gwine to tell you about the affecting partin I had with my congregation at Bethel Chapel. Arter I had got through with my farewell sarmont, as I come down outen the pulpit, the old gray-headed breethern and sisters who had listened to my voice for twenty years crowded around me and with sobbing voices and tearful eyes said, 'Farewell, Brother Crafford!'

"As I walked down the aisle, the young ladies—tricked out in their finery of brass jewelry, geegaws, jimcracks, paint, and flounces—looked up with their bright eyes and pronounced with their rosy lips, 'Farewell, Brother Crafford!'

"The young men in their tight patent leather boots, high collars, and flashy waistcosts—smelling of pomatum and cigar smoke—with their Shanghai coats and striped zebra pants—they, too, said 'Farewell, Brother Crafford!'

"The little children—lambs in the field—lifted up their tiny hands and small voices and with one accord said, 'Farewell, Brother Crafford!'

"The colored breethern of the congregation now came

forward (black sheep who had been admitted to the fold under my ministry) with tears rolling down their sable cheeks—they, too, said 'Farewell, Brother Crafford!'

"As I got on my horse and bade adieu to my congregation forever, I turned to take a last look at the old church where I had preached the unsarchable riches of religion for mor'n twenty years, and as I gazed at its dilapidated walls and moss-covered roof, it, too, seemed to say, 'Farewell, Brother Crafford!'

"As I rode down through the village, the people who poked their heads outen the winders and the servants who lent on their brooms—all seemed to say, 'Farewell, Brother Crafford!'

"Crossing a little creek that was gurgling and singing over its pebbly bed as it rejoiced on its way to the great ocean of eternity—it, too, seemed to say, 'Farewell, Brother Crafford!'

"As I rode along down a hot, dusty lane, an old sow that was asleep in a fence corner jumped out of a suddent with a loud broo-oo, broo-oo—she, too, seemed to say, 'Farewell, Brother Crafford!'

"My horse, he got frightened and jumped from under me, and as he curled his tail over his back, kicked up his heels and ran off—he, too, seemed to say, 'Farewell, Brother Crafford!'"

2

Preachers love to travel, sometimes taking their parish-ioners along with them on pilgrimages to the Holy Land or to Nashville. Globe-trotting clerics are no new phenomenon, as this mid-nineteenth century poem shows. The well-travelled parson is able, through his travels, to sprinkle his sermons with exotic European references, both to the pleasure and the consternation of his congregation.

"OUR TRAVELLED PARSON"

Will Carleton

For twenty years and over, our good parson had been toiling,
To chip the bad meat from our hearts, and keep the good from spoiling;
But suddenly he wilted down, and went to looking sickly,
And the doctor said that something must be put up for him quickly.
So we kind o' clubbed together, each according to his notion,
And bought a circular ticket, in the lands across the ocean;
Wrapped some pocket-money in it—what we thought would easy do him—
And appointed me committee-man, to go and take it to him.
I found him in his study, looking rather worse than ever;
And told him 'twas decided that his flock and he should sever.
Then his eyes grew big with wonder, and it seemed almost to blind 'em,
And some tears looked out o' window, with some others close behind 'em!
But I handed him the ticket, with a little bow of deference,

And he studied quite a little ere he got the proper reference,
and then the tears that waited—great unmanageable
creatures—
Let themselves quite out o' window, and came climbing down
his features.

I wish you could ha' seen him when he came back, fresh and
glowing,
His clothes all worn and seedy, and his face all fat and
knowing;
I wish you could ha' heard him, when he prayed for us who
sent him,
Paying back with compound int'rest every dollar that we'd
lent him!
'Twas a feast to true believers—'twas a blight on contradic-
tion—
To hear one just from Calvary talk about the crucifixion;
'Twas a damper on those fellows who pretended they could
doubt it,
To have a man who'd been there stand and tell 'em all about it!
Why every foot of Scripture, whose location used to stump us,
Was now regularly laid out with the different points o'
compass;
When he undertook a subject, in what nat'ral lines he'd draw
it!
He would paint it out so honest that it seemed as if you saw it.
And the way he went for Europe! oh, the way he scampered
through it!
Not a mountain but he clim' it—not a city but he knew it;
There wasn't any subject to explain, in all creation,
But he could go to Europe, and bring back an illustration!
So we crowded out to hear him, quite instructed and
delighted;
'Twas a picture-show, a lecture, and a sermon—all united;
And my wife would rub her glasses, and serenely pet her
Test'ment,

And whisper, "That ere ticket was a splendid good
    investment."

Now, after six months' travel, we was most of us all ready
To settle down a little, so's to live more staid and steady;
To develop home resources, with no foreign cares to fret us,
Using house-made faith more frequent; but our parson
    wouldn't let us!
To view the same old scenery, time and time again he'd call
    us—
Over rivers, plains, and mountains he would any minute haul
    us;
He slighted our soul-sorrows, and our spirits' aches and
    ailings,
To get the cargo ready for his regular Sunday sailings!
Why, he'd take us off a-touring, in all spiritual weather,
Till we at last got home-sick and sea-sick all together!
And "I wish to all that's peaceful," said one free-expressioned
    brother,
"That the Lord had made one cont'nent, an' then never made
    another!"

Sometimes, indeed, he'd take us into old, familiar places,
And pull along quite nat'ral, in the good old Gospel traces:
But soon my wife would shudder, just as if a chill had got her,
Whispering, "Oh my goodness gracious! he's a-takin' to the
    water!"
And it wasn't the same old comfort, when he called around to
    see us;
On some branch of foreign travel he was sure at last to tree us;
All unconscious of his error, he would sweetly patronise us,
And with oft-repeated stories still endeavor to surprise us.

And the sinners got to laughing; and that finally galled and
    stung us,
To ask him, wouldn't he kindly once more settle down among
    us?

Didn't he think that more home produce would improve our
   soul's digestions?
They appointed me committee-man to go and ask the
   questions.
I found him in his garden, trim an' buoyant as a feather;
He shook my hand, exclaiming, "This is quite Italian
   weather!"
How it 'minds me of the evenings when, your distant hearts
   caressing,
Upon my dear good brothers, I invoked God's choicest
   blessing!"

I went and told the brothers, "No; I cannot bear to grieve him;
He's so happy in his exile, it's the proper place to leave him.
I took that journey to him, and right bitterly I rue it;
But I cannot take it from him; if *you* want to, go and do it."

Now a new restraint entirely seemed next Sunday to enfold
   him,
And he looked so hurt and humbled, that I knew that they had
   told him,
Subdued-like was his manner, and some tones were hardly
   vocal;
But every word and sentence was pre-eminently local!
Still, the sermon sounded awkward, and we awkward felt who
   heard it;
'Twas a grief to see him steer it—'twas a pain to hear him word
   it.
"When I was abroad"—was maybe half-a-dozen times
   repeated;
But that sentence seemed to choke him, and was always
   uncompleted.
As weeks went on, his old smile would occasionally brighten,
But the voice was growing feeble, and the face began to
   whiten;
He would look off to the eastward, with a wistful, weary
   sighing.

And 'twas whispered that our pastor in a foreign land was
  dying.
The coffin lay 'mid garlands, smiling sad as if they knew us;
The patient face within it preached a final sermon to us;
Our parson *had* gone touring—on a trip he'd long been
  earning—
In that wonderland, whence tickets are not issued for
  returning!
O tender, good heart-shepherd! your sweet smiling lips,
  half-parted,
Told of scenery that burst on you, just the minute that you
  started!
Could you preach once more among us, you might wander,
  without fearing;
You could give us tales of glory that we'd never tire of hearing!

3

As a brilliant and witty interpreter of the Christian faith, Cambridge professor C. S. Lewis is known as one of the twentieth century's foremost Christian apologists. His Screwtape Letters *were his first major effort at humor with a sermonic purpose. In that book, a young devil corresponds with an older one concerning the practical aspects of the corruption of humanity.*

In The Great Divorce, *Lewis takes a load of assorted ghosts on a fantastic bus ride from a dingy gray town (Hell) to a strange new land (Heaven) peopled by Bright People. Once there, one of the ghosts (a pompous, free-thinking bishop) has a revealing conversation with one of heaven's Bright People, with whom he once discussed theology in his former life.*

Through this conversation, Lewis makes fun of modern, compromised Christianity and its intellectual pretensions once it is confronted with the odd fact that the claims of orthodox Christianity just might be true.

By the time the bus leaves Heaven to return some of its passengers to Hell, we have every reason to believe that our bloated bishop will be on board.

"THE BISHOP FROM HELL"*

From *The Great Divorce*

C. S. Lewis

C lose beside me I saw another of the bright people in conversation with a ghost. It was that fat ghost with the

*From *The Great Divorce* by C.S. Lewis. Copyright © 1946 by Collins Publishers. Used with permission.

cultured voice who had addressed me in the bus, and it seemed to be wearing gaiters.

"My dear boy, I'm delighted to see you," it was saying to the Spirit, who was naked and almost blindingly white. "I was talking to your poor father the other day and wondering where you were."

"You didn't bring him?" said the other.

"Well, no. He lives a long way from the bus, and, to be quite frank, he's been getting a little eccentric lately. A little difficult. Losing his grip. He never was prepared to make any great efforts, you know. If you remember, he used to go to sleep when you and I got talking seriously! Ah, Dick, I shall never forget some of our talks. I expect you've changed your views a bit since then. You became rather narrow-minded towards the end of your life: but no doubt you've broadened out again."

"How do you mean?"

"Well, it's obvious by now, isn't it, that you weren't quite right. Why, my dear boy, you were coming to believe in a literal Heaven and Hell!"

"But wasn't I right?"

"Oh, in a spiritual sense, to be sure. I still believe in them in that way. I am still, my dear boy, looking for the Kingdom. But nothing superstitious or mythological. . . . "

"Excuse me. Where do you imagine you've been?"

"Ah, I see. You mean that the grey town with its continual hope of morning (we must all live by hope, must we not?), with its field for indefinite progress, is, in a sense, Heaven, if only we have eyes to see it? That is a beautiful idea."

"I didn't mean that at all. Is it possible you don't know where you've been?"

"Now that you mention it, I don't think we ever did give it a name. What do you call it?"

"We call it Hell."

"There is no need to be profane, my dear boy. I may not be very orthodox, in your sense of that word, but I do feel that these matters ought to be discussed simply, and seriously, and reverently."

"Discuss Hell *reverently*? I meant what I said. You have been in Hell: though if you don't go back you may call it Purgatory."

"Go on, my dear boy, go on. That is *so* like you. No doubt you'll tell me why, on your view, I was sent there. I'm not angry."

"But don't you know? You went there because you are an apostate."

"Are you serious, Dick?"

"Perfectly."

"This is worse than I expected. Do you really think people are penalised for their honest opinions? Even assuming, for the sake of argument, that those opinions were mistaken."

"Do you really think there are no sins of intellect?"

"There are indeed, Dick. There is hidebound prejudice, and intellectual dishonesty, and timidity, and stagnation. But honest opinions fearlessly followed—they are not sins."

"I know we used to talk that way. I did it too until the end of my life when I became what you call narrow. It all turns on what are honest opinions.

"Mine certainly were. They were not only honest but heroic. I asserted them fearlessly. When the doctrine of the Resurrection ceased to commend itself to the critical faculties which God had given me, I openly rejected it. I preached my famous sermon. I defied the whole chapter. I took every risk."

"What risk? What was at all likely to come of it except what actually came—popularity, sales for your books, invitations, and finally a bishopric?"

"Dick, this is unworthy of you. What are you suggesting?"

"Friend, I am not suggesting at all. You see, I *know* now. Let us be frank. Our opinions were not honestly come by. We simply found ourselves in contact with a certain current of ideas and plunged into it because it seemed modern and successful. At College, you know, we just started automatically writing the kinds of essays that got good marks and saying the kinds of things that won applause. When, in our whole lives, did we honestly face, in solitude, the one question on which all turned: whether after all the Supernatural might not in fact occur? When did we put up one moment's real resistance to the loss of our faith?"

"If this is meant to be a sketch of the genesis of liberal theology in general, I reply that it is a mere libel. Do you suggest that men like . . . "

"I have nothing to do with any generality. Nor with any man but me and you. Oh, as you love your own soul, remember. You know that you and I were playing with loaded dice. We didn't *want* the other to be true. We were afraid of crude salavationism, afraid of a breach with the spirit of the age, afraid of ridicule, afraid (above all) of real spiritual fears and hopes."

"I'm far from denying that young men may make mistakes. They may well be influenced by current fashions of thought. But it's not a question of how the opinions are formed. The point is that they were my honest opinions, sincerely expressed."

"Of course. Having allowed oneself to drift, unresisting, unpraying, accepting every half-conscious solicitation from our desires, we reached a point where we no longer believed the Faith. Just in the same way, a jealous man, drifting and unresisting, reaches a point at which he believes lies about his best friend: a drunkard reaches a point at which (for the moment) he actually believes that another glass will do him no harm. The beliefs are sincere in the sense that they do occur as psychological events in the man's mind. If that's what you mean by sincerity they are sincere, and so were ours. But errors which are sincere in that sense are not innocent."

"You'll be justifying the Inquisition in a moment!"

"Why? Because the Middle Ages erred in one direction, does it follow that there is no error in the opposite direction?"

"Well, this is extremely interesting," said the Episcopal

31

Ghost. "It's a point of view. Certainly, it's a point of view. In the meantime . . . "

"There is no meantime," replied the other. "All that is over. We are not playing now. I have been talking of the past (your past and mine) only in order that you may turn from it forever. One wrench and the tooth will be out. You can begin as if nothing had ever gone wrong. White as snow. It's all true, you know. He is in me, for you, with that power. And—I have come a long journey to meet you. You have seen Hell: you are in sight of Heaven. Will you, even now, repent and believe?"

"I'm not sure that I've got the exact point you are trying to make," said the Ghost.

"I am not trying to make any point," said the Spirit. "I am telling you to repent and believe."

"But my dear boy, I believe already. We may not be perfectly agreed, but you have completely misjudged me if you do not realise that my religion is a very real and a very precious thing to me."

"Very well," said the other, as if changing his plan. "Will you believe in *me?*"

"In what sense?"

"Will you come with me to the mountains? It will hurt at first, until your feet are hardened. Reality is harsh to the feet of shadows. But will you come?"

"Well, that is a plan. I am perfectly ready to consider it. Of course I should require some assurances. . . . I should want a guarantee that you are taking me to a place where I shall find a wider sphere of usefulness—and scope for the talents that God has given me—and an atmosphere of free inquiry—in short, all that one means by civilisation and—er—the spiritual life."

"No," said the other. "I can promise you none of these things. No sphere of usefulness: you are not needed there at all. No scope for your talents: only forgiveness for having perverted them. No atmosphere of inquiry, for I will bring you to the land not of questions but of answers, and you shall see the face of God."

"Ah, but we must all interpret those beautiful words in our own way! For me there is no such thing as a final answer. The free wind of inquiry must *always* continue to blow through the mind, must it not? 'Prove all things' . . . to travel hopefully is better than to arrive."

"If that were true, and known to be true, how could anyone travel hopefully? There would be nothing to hope for."

"But you must feel yourself that there is something stifling about the idea of finality? Stagnation, my dear boy, what is more soul destroying than stagnation?"

"You think that, because hitherto you have experienced truth only with the abstract intellect. I will bring you where you can taste it like honey and be embraced by it as by a bridegroom. Your thirst shall be quenched."

"Well, really, you know, I am not aware of a thirst for some ready-made truth which puts an end to intellectual activity in the way you seem to be describing. Will it leave me the free play of Mind, Dick? I must insist on that, you know."

"Free, as a man is free to drink while he is drinking. He is not free still to be dry." The Ghost seemed to think for a moment. "I can make nothing of that idea," it said.

"Listen!" said the White Spirit. "Once you were a child. Once you knew what inquiry was for. There was a time when you asked questions because you wanted answers, and were glad when you had found them. Become that child again: even now."

"Ah, but when I became a man I put away childish things."

"You have gone far wrong. Thirst was made for water; inquiry for truth. What you now call the free play of inquiry has neither more nor less to do with the ends for which intelligence was given you than masturbation has to do with marriage."

"If you cannot be reverent, there is at least no need to be obscene. The suggestion that I should return at my age to the mere factual inquisitiveness of boyhood strikes me as preposterous. In any case, that question-and-answer conception of thought only applies to matters of fact. Religious and speculative questions are surely on a different level."

"We know nothing of religion here: we think only of Christ. We know nothing of speculation. Come and see. I will bring you to Eternal Fact, the Father of all other facthood."

"I should object very strongly to describing God as a 'fact.' The Supreme Value would surely be a less inadequate description. It is hardly . . . "

"Do you not even believe that He exists?"

"Exists? What does Existence mean?" You *will* keep on implying some sort of static, ready-made reality which is, so to speak, 'there,' and to which our minds have simply to conform. These great mysteries cannot be approached in that way. If there were such a thing (there is no need to interrupt, my dear boy) quite frankly, I should not be interested in it. It would be of no *religious* significance. God, for me, is something purely spiritual. The spirit of sweetness and light and tolerance—and, er, service, Dick, service. We mustn't forget that, you know."

"If the thirst of the Reason is really dead . . . ," said the Spirit, and then stopped as though pondering. Then suddenly he said, "Can you, at least, still desire happiness?"

"Happiness, my dear Dick," said the Ghost placidly, "happiness, as you will come to see when you are older, lies in the path of duty. Which reminds me . . . Bless my soul, I'd nearly forgotten. Of course I can't come with you. I have to be back next Friday to read a paper. We have a little Theological Society down there. Oh yes! there is plenty of intellectual life. Not of a very high quality, perhaps. One notices a certain lack of grip—a certain confusion of mind. That is where I can be of some use to them. There are even regrettable jealousies. . . . I don't know why, but tempers seem less controlled than they used to be. Still, one mustn't expect too much of human nature. I feel I can do a great work among them. But you've never asked me what my paper is about! I'm taking the text about growing up to the measure of the stature of Christ and working out an idea which I feel sure you'll be interested in. I'm going to point out how people always forget that Jesus (here the Ghost bowed) was a comparatively young man when he died. He would have outgrown some of his earlier views, you know, if he'd lived. As he might have done, with a little more tact and patience. I am going to ask my audience to consider what his mature views would have been. A profoundly interesting question. What a different Christianity we might have had if only the Founder had reached his full stature! I shall end up by pointing out how this deepens the significance of the Crucifixion. One feels for the first time what a disaster it was: what a tragic waste . . . so much promise cut short. Oh, must you be going? Well, so must I. Goodbye, my dear boy. It has been a great pleasure. Most stimulating and provocative. Goodbye, goodbye, goodbye."

The Ghost nodded its head and beamed on the Spirit with a bright clerical smile—or with the best approach to it which such unsubstantial lips could manage—and then turned away humming softly to itself "City of God, how broad and far."

4

Millions of European readers have loved the charming little world of don Camillo. He is the creation of Italian humorist Giovanni Guareschi, who set don Camillo in his native Parma—an Italian region whose inhabitants are noted for the warmth of their humor and the fire of their political passions. Both qualities are evident in this account of don Camillo's baptismal confrontation with a Marxist. Guareschi's humor has not only brought him much fame and success, but also has landed him in prison on at least two occasions for making fun of Italian politicians!

"A BAPTISM"*

Giovanni Guareschi

One day Don Camillo, perched high on a ladder, was busily polishing St. Joseph's halo. Unexpectedly a man and two women, one of whom was Peppone's wife, came into the church. Don Camillo turned around to ask what they wanted.

"There is something here to be baptized," replied the man, and one of the women held up a bundle containing a baby.

"Whose is it?" inquired Don Camillo, coming down from his ladder.

"Mine," replied Peppone's wife.

"And your husband's?" persisted Don Camillo.

"Well, naturally! Who else would be the father? You, maybe?" retorted Peppone's wife indignantly.

"No need to be offended," observed Don Camillo on his

*From *The Little World of don Camillo* by Giovannino Guareschi. Copyright © 1950. Used with permission.

way to the sacristy. "I've been told often enough that your party approves of free love."

As he passed before the high altar Don Camillo knelt down and gave a discreet wink in the direction of Christ. "Did you hear that one?" he murmured with a happy grin. "One in the eye for the Godless ones!"

"Don't talk rubbish, Don Camillo," replied Christ irritably. "If they had no God why should they come here to get their child baptized? If Peppone's wife had boxed your ears it would have served you right."

"If Peppone's wife had boxed my ears I should have taken the three of them by the scruff of their necks and . . . "

"And what?" Christ asked severely.

"Oh, nothing; just a figure of speech," Don Camillo hastened to assure Him, rising to his feet.

"Don Camillo, watch your step," Christ said sternly.

Duly vested, Don Camillo approached the baptismal font. "What do you wish to name this child?" he asked Peppone's wife.

"Lenin, Libero, Antonio," she replied.

"Then go and get him baptized in Russia," said Don Camillo calmly, replacing the cover on the font.

The priest's hands were as big as shovels and the three left the church without protest. But as Don Camillo tried to slip into the sacristy he was stopped by the voice of Christ. "Don Camillo, you have done a very wicked thing. Go at once and bring those people back and baptize their child."

"But, Lord," protested Don Camillo, "You really must bear in mind that baptism is a very sacred matter. Baptism is . . . "

"Don Camillo," Christ interrupted him, "are you trying to teach me the nature of baptism? Didn't I invent it? I tell you that you have been guilty of gross presumption, because if that child were to die at this moment it would be your fault if it failed to attain Paradise!"

"Lord, let us not be melodramatic! Why in the name of Heaven should it die? It's as pink and white as a rose!"

"That doesn't mean a thing!" Christ pointed out. "What if a tile should fall on its head or it suddenly had convulsions? It was your duty to baptize it."

Don Camillo raised his hands in protest. "But, Lord, think it over. If it were certain that the child would go to Hell, then we might stretch a point. But since he might easily manage to slip into Heaven, in spite of his father, how can You ask me to risk anyone getting in there with a name like Lenin? I'm thinking of the reputation of Heaven."

"The reputation of Heaven is my business," shouted Christ angrily. "What matters to me is that a man should be a decent fellow, and I care less than nothing whether his name be Lenin or Button. At the very most, you should have pointed out to those people that saddling children with fantastic names may be a nuisance to them when they grow up."

"Very well," replied Don Camillo. "I am always wrong. I'll see what I can do."

Just then someone came into the church. It was Peppone, alone, with the baby in his arms. He closed the church door behind him and bolted it. "I'm not leaving this church," he said, "until my son has been baptized with the name that I have chosen."

"Look at that," whispered Don Camillo, smiling as he turned to Christ. "Now do you see what these people are? One is filled with the holiest intentions, and this is how they treat you."

"Put yourself in his place," Christ replied. "One may not approve of his attitude but one can understand it."

Don Camillo shook his head.

"I have already said that I do not leave this place unless you baptize my son!" repeated Peppone. After laying the bundle containing the baby upon a bench he took off his coat, rolled up his sleeves, and came toward the priest threateningly.

"Lord," implored Don Camillo. "I ask You! If You think one of Your priests should give way to the threats of a layman, then I must obey. But if I do and tomorrow they bring me a calf and compel me to baptize it, You must not complain. You know very well how dangerous it is to create precedents."

"All right, but in this case you must try to make him understand . . . "

"And if he hits me?"

"Then you must accept it. You must endure and suffer as I did."

Don Camillo turned to his visitor. "Very well, Peppone," he said. "The baby will leave the church baptized, but not with that accursed name."

"Don Camillo," stuttered Peppone, "don't forget that my stomach has never recovered from that bullet I stopped in the mountains. If you hit low I go after you with a bench."

"Don't worry, Peppone, I can deal with you entirely in the upper stories," Don Camillo assured him, landing a quick one above his ear.

They were both burly men and their blows whistled through the air. After twenty minutes of speechless and furious combat, Don Camillo distinctly heard a voice behind him.

"Now, Don Camillo! A left to the jaw!" It came from Christ above the altar. Don Camillo struck hard and Peppone crashed to the ground. He remained there for about ten minutes; then he sat up, got to his feet, rubbed his jaw, shook himself, put on his jacket and reknotted his red handkerchief. Then he picked up the baby. Fully vested, Don Camillo was waiting, steady as a rock, beside the font. Peppone approached him slowly.

"What are we going to name him?" asked Don Camillo.

"Camillo, Libero, Antonio," muttered Peppone.

Don Camillo shook his head. "No; we will name him Libero, Camillo, Lenin," he said. "After all, the Camillo will cancel out Lenin any day."

"Amen," muttered Peppone, still massaging his jaw.

When all was done and Don Camillo passed before the altar, Christ smiled and remarked: "Don Camillo, I have to admit that in politics you are my master."

"And in boxing," replied Don Camillo with perfect gravity, carelessly fingering a large lump on his forehead.

5

For over a decade, The Wittenburg Door has been the leading religious humor magazine in the United States. Founded by a group of young evangelicals, The Door finds fun in almost everything sacred, all in the interest of one of the most sacred gifts of all—the gift of laughter.

In the first selection, Patrick Heston gives a quick history of "The Reformers" seen through the eyes of a somnambulant seminarian, followed by a Final Exam. Who says that history ought to be dull?

The second sample of The Door *is one of my own, "Taking the Fun Out of Fundies." I tell the incident just as it happened—more or less. Who says that disputes between Christians ought to be dull?*

SELECTIONS FROM *THE WITTENBURG DOOR*

"THE REFORMERS: A HISTORY OF THE REFORMATION"*

From the Notes of a Sleepy Student

Patrick C. Heston

T he stage was now set, and with the emergence of four great reformers, the reformation was in full bloom.

MARTIN LUTHER

Martin Luther was a translator of the Bible, a composer of catechisms, a developer of liturgies,[1] a believer in devils and

*Used with permission of the author.
[1] As well as "biggergies."

witches, a man who threw inkwells at shadows on the wall, and was such an integral and beloved part of his monastic order that he was sent to Rome in 1510 to buy onions.

Some called him "Martin," others, "a drunken German." Luther did thoroughly enjoy his beer. But, as we shall see shortly, the Pope would have enjoyed Luther's bier.

Luther's road to problems with the Pope—as well as his road out of Catholicism—commenced while on a pilgrimage to Rome on behalf of his monastic order. As he was climbing up Pilate's steps, kissing each one and repeating aloud something about Knobnoster, Missouri, he asked the question: "Who knows whether it is so?"[2] At the end of his pilgrimage, he remarked that he had gone to Rome for onions and returned with garlic. Which, by the way, no doubt disturbed the monastery cook[3] who had asked specifically for onions.

Afterwards, there was nothing for Luther to do but earn his TH.D. degree from a university with much Erfurt. This he did in spite of being called into the Dean of Students' office on numerous occasions for so-called "boyish pranks." The most notable of these pranks occurred on October 31, 1517. On that night, Luther took ninety-five doctoral theses from the university library and nailed them all over the Castle Church in Wittenberg. Little did he know at the time that such a simple Halloween stunt would start a chain reaction which would upset the whole of Catholicism.

So incensed was the Pope that he sent a bull[4] after Luther. The bull's name was "Exsurge Domine." It took the bull a full three months to find Luther.[5] The bull, obviously more gifted in speech than in manhunting, called Luther "a wild boar who had invaded the vineyard."[6] The bull then gave Luther sixty days to turn from his heretical course. When the sixty days

---

[2]Presumably, whether or not there is such a place as Knobnoster, Missouri.

[3]Food Friar.

[4]Some of this figuratively, with reference to all the Pope was saying (about Luther) being a bunch of.

[5]A bloodhound would have been more efficient, but a bull more intimidating.

[6]In light of such a comment, it is probable that this bull was looking for someone else—say, an animal.

were up, and it being December,[7] Luther burned the bull and ate it.

Shortly thereafter, Luther discovered that Pope Leo X had approved the selling of indulgences[8] to complete the building of the magnificent new St. Peter's. Needing money desperately, Leo X sent several papal people to sell these indulgences. These agents of the Pope were led by Oral Tetzel, a specialist in fundraising, who claimed God would strike him dead if he did not raise eight million dollars by early spring.

Luther felt that the sale of indulgences by the Church—and many more "religious" practices—were wrong and, in 1519, publicly debated Catholic theologians at Leipfrog. During the debate, Luther stated that the Pope ruled on human, not divine (not even humane), authority.

The Pope was so upset at these comments that he charged Luther with heresy. But it did no good because of a turn in political events.

On January 12, 1519, the Emperor of the Holy Roman Empire, Maximilian, died. The vacant office was elective. Any ruler in the world could seek it. The choice finally came down to two men: Charles of Spain and Francis of France. The Pope liked neither one and threw his support behind Frederick the Wise of Saxony. But Frederick defeated himself by casting his vote for Charles of Spain,[9] who became Charles V of the Holy Roman Empire. As it turned out, Charles V liked Martin Luther and would do nothing about the Pope's charge of heresy.

But the charges against Martin Luther became so intense and severe that Charles V decided to give him a hearing at "The Emperor's First Diet." By modern standards, this well-advertised, gala event was quite high in calories. The Emperor's diet consisted of seven electors, lesser princes,[10] and representatives from all the free cities. Obviously not losing weight, Charles switched next time to a diet of worms.

---

[7]When heat was needed and food was scarce.

[8]Sixteenth century Bingo.

[9]Hereafter, people stopped calling Frederick "the Wise."

[10]The more the Emperor ate, the lesser and lesser there were.

At the diet—the Emperor obviously not in a good mood—Luther was called an outlaw and a heretic. But, in the confusion of flying charges, he fled for protection to the Castle of the Elector of Saxony. There, he lived for almost a year under the disguise of "Knight George."[11]

In the years that followed, Martin Luther became so popular through his writings that some Princes in Germany actually formed a Lutheran Party. From this small and humble beginning would come Lutheranism and, in 1955, the declaration of Lutheranism as the "state religion."[12]

The Emperor's next diet was in 1530—this time in Augsburg.[13] There, Luther confessed his sins and wrongs against the Catholic Church. This became known as the "Augsburg Confession."

After this confession, the Pope was satisfied—even more so when Luther died sixteen years later.

HULDRYCH ZWINGLI

Huldrych Zwingli was born January 1, 1484, in Wildhaus in The Toggenburg, Sanki Gallen, Switzerland. He was eighteen before he could write his address. His father was a chief magistrate, and his uncle, Bartholomew, had invented (and then given his name to) a recent creation called a Zwing set.

Zwingli led an interesting life. He served as chaplain to Swiss mercenaries in Italy and, nine years later, led the opposition against mercenary service. In 1522, he approved the eating of meat during Lent, one year later published his sixty-seven theses and, on January 5, 1527, approved the drowning of Felix Manz for practicing re-baptism.[14] After this event, the Anabaptists began practicing sprinkling.

Needless to say, by the time Zwingli reached his mid-forties, everybody wanted a piece of him. His home base

---

[11]Years later, the disguise was used again, this time called "Boy George."

[12]The most famous state being Missouri.

[13]Why the Emperor kept going somewhere else for his diet is unknown, but it gave rise to the phrase "going on a diet."

[14]The assumption being that if they kept Felix under long enough, he would not need to be rebaptized.

of Zurich was attacked in 1531 and Huldrych was killed—his body being cut into four pieces[15] and thrown into the fire (not quite as he had requested).

JOHN CALVIN

John "is anybody happy" Calvin was born in Noyon, France in 1509 and was educated at the University of Paris, where he graduated with a Doctor of Laws degree in 1532.

In 1533, King Francis I began persecuting heretics. Calvin, not yet aware he was one, sensed no danger. But, within a few months, he had to flee Paris for Basel with his friend Nicholas Cop. Cop's most famous sermon had attacked the Church as well as the renowned Paris theologians. Calvin had a hand in writing the sermon,[16] and had to run for his life to escape royal punishment, having raised a royal blush.

Suddenly aware that he was a religious heretic, Calvin decided to experience a religious conversion, which he did in 1534. During the next two years, he traveled widely in France and regularly checked in and out of an Institute for Religious Christians—the pressure, at times, being too much.

Eventually, he settled in Geneva, a city steeped in sin and decadence. Every third house was a tavern.[17] The red-light district was frequented regularly by the population. To correct the latter situation, Calvin posted a special watch[18] to keep people away from the red-light sector of town. It so affected the city that Calvin was driven out, exiled to Strassburg. As the years passed by, Calvin was begged often to return to Geneva.[19] Finally, on September 13, 1541, he did.

Shortly after his return, he began once again to institute his positive approach to community problem solving. He approved the death sentence for Servetus, drove the

---

[15]To satisfy all who wanted one.
[16]Nonetheless, his entire body had to flee.
[17]But, who was counting?
[18]A Swiss watch.
[19]Mostly by residents of Strassburg.

Libertines out of town, and used spies and police tactics to search out and punish people who were breaching the laws of the Church.

Calvin established heavy fines and penalties for such ghastly and immoral horrors as: being absent from or critiquing sermons; laughing during Church services; wearing bright colors; being unable to recite prayers; playing cards;[20] marrying your daughter to a Catholic; and saying the Pope was a good man.

In spite of such reforms, Calvin spent his last years in Geneva being insulted in the streets, threatened by thugs who wished to throw him in the river, sung to by large crowds gathered outside his home singing obscene lyrics, and shot at during the night.

He died on May 27, 1564—A Geneva holiday.[21]

JOHN KNOX

John Knox was born near Edinburgh, Scotland, in 1513. Some scholars assign his birth to 1505, but John probably knew more about it than they. His father, Hard, had started a school which exists yet to this day.

After being ordained a priest and later experiencing a spiritual awakening, John Knox began associating with a Protestant leader named George Wishart. But, when Wishart was tried for heresy and burned at the stake, Knox felt it was time to get back into the Catholic camp. That is, until some Protestant rebels retaliated by assassinating a leading Catholic churchman. At this time, Knox felt it was best to run for it.

He fled to the Castle of St. Andrews where he became chaplain to a band of refugees and rebels. But, in 1547, Catholic forces, aided by the French, attacked the Castle. Knox and his companions were captured and imprisoned.[22]

Knox's imprisonment was on a French warship, where he

---

[20]Except Rook.

[21]This was not a holiday prior to Calvin's death.

[22]Knox had no one to blame but himself. When the Catholics knocked at the door, shouting, "Knox! Knox!," the Scottish Reformer answered, "Who's there?"

was chained in a galley and forced to pull oars.[23] It was there that he held his first warship service.

Released in 1549, Knox returned to England, only to be declared an outlaw by Mary of Guise, the Scottish regent, ten years later. When Mary died, Knox was arrested for treason, only to be released when Queen Mary of England abdicated her throne. Thoroughly confused by this time, Knox retired to Scotland where he started a Gelatin company before suffering a paralytic stroke and dying two years later.

FINAL EXAM

1. If followers of Martin Luther are called Lutherans, should followers of John Bunyan be called Bunyans?
2. Why did Luther raise such a beef over a bull?
3. Is it true, as many scholars have suggested, that the Catholic theologians at Leipfrog kept jumping from one issue to the other in their debate with Luther?
4. Was Frederick the Wise, wise? Was Francis of France, frank?
5. Say Huldrych Zwingli fast three times.
6. Is Calvin loved as much today as when he was alive? Would you hire him at your church?
7. History informs us that John Knox had several run-ins with Mary of Guise. This being the case, and he being such a great preacher, why couldn't he reformer?

"TAKING THE FUN OUT OF FUNDIES"

William H. Willimon

One of the hazards of serving a church in Greenville, South Carolina, is that one has to put up with the presence of Bob Jones University—"The World's Most Unusual University."

-----

[23]Which was especially difficult while chained in the galley. Nor do we know where he was supposed to pull these oars to.

When Bishop Tullis moved me to Greenville my friends said they would give me six months before I would be in hot water with the folks at Dr. Bob's school. In scarcely three months I had already had my first tiff with them over their dispute with the Internal Revenue Service. It seems that the I.R.S. wanted to take away Dr. Bob's tax exempt status because he had rules against interracial dating among his students. Ironically, I said that this was none of the I.R.S.'s business. It is not up to the tax people to judge what is a "valid religious belief." I simply said, in an interview with the *Greenville News*, that the I.R.S. ought to lay off the good Dr. Jones. "This is a free country," I said. "The Constitution guarantees that anybody can make a fool out of himself in the name of religion and get away with it. If Dr. Jones wants to give us Christians a bad name because of his racist attitudes, that's our problem, not the government's."

It seems that Dr. Jones was neither amused nor gratified by my support. In one of his evening chapel talks on his radio station he called me "a liar, a liberal, a Communist, and an apostate." That's gratitude for you. A few weeks later when Dr. Bob called upon the Lord to "smite Alexander Haig, hip and thigh," I decided not to have anything else to say about Dr. Jones or his racist school—he plays dirty.

One of my members, upon hearing that Dr. Jones had labeled me an "apostate" said, "We suspected our preacher of being a Democrat but I didn't know anything about him being an 'apostate.' Is that some kind of perversion?" With as little theology as we Methodists have to start with, it is tough for us to become apostates. At any rate, this was the setting of a telephone call which I received about a week after Dr. Jones called me dirty names in a sermon.

HIM: "Hello, Dr. Willimon? This is Dean So-and-So of Bob Jones University. How are you tonight?"

ME: "Fine, at least I think I am."

HIM: "Good. Dr. Willimon, I was interested in your remarks about our school in the newspaper recently.

I gathered, from reading your remarks, that you may not know much about our school. Perhaps you don't understand our programs, our goals."

ME: "Possibly. However, I was born in Greenville, lived here most of my life, so I have followed Dr. Jones and his machinations for many years. I may know more about him than you do."

HIM: "Well, er, uh, that may be but, Dr. Willimon, can we have a Christian-to-Christian talk?"

ME: "*I* can."

HIM: "Now Dr. Willimon, you believe in the Bible don't you?"

ME: "I certainly do."

HIM: "Of course. Well, Bob Jones University is founded and operated on strictly Biblical principles. Take, for instance, our policies on the mixing of the races."

ME: "Yes, let's take them."

HIM: "Well, they are based on strictly Biblical principles, on Biblical teaching."

ME: "I doubt that. I expect that they are based on Dr. Jones' personal opinions of what is right—as are many of your rules there."

HIM: "Now look here. (pause) Dr. Willimon, you have a family?"

ME: "Yes, I do."

HIM: "Do you have a daughter?" (At this point I knew what was coming. After all, I wasn't born and bred in South Carolina for nothing.)

ME: "I do."

HIM: "Well, how would you like for your own daughter to marry a black man?"

ME: "I wouldn't like it at all."

HIM: "Right, you wouldn't like it. Now, all our racial policies are trying to do is to support the very principles which you yourself believe in."

ME: "I wouldn't want my daughter to marry a *white* man. I wouldn't want her to marry *any* man. She is only five years old. Is Dr. Jones advocating little girls getting married to old men? I think that's sick. That's disgusting. Where does he get that out of the Bible? I think that's . . ."

HIM: "No, no. I meant that when she grows up, would you like her to marry a black man?"

ME: "Just the thought of it, my little, tiny daughter getting married. That's awful. Dr. Jones has some nerve calling *me* a Communist. I am going to condemn him from my pulpit next Sunday. It's a sin, a perversion! Little girls getting married before they even get a chance to be in kindergarten! It's an outrage!"

HIM: (Now shouting into the telephone.) "Would you listen to me! I am trying to tell you, if you'll just keep your mouth shut, that I was saying that, when your daughter got older, say twenty-five or so . . ."

ME: "Look, you stop talking about my daughter. You and Dr. Jones. Keep your hands off of her, you dirty old . . ."

HIM: "I can't believe that you are a minister of the Gospel. I can't believe that those people over at that church, even a *Methodist* church, put up with a preacher like you."

ME: "You've got your nerve calling me a disgrace. At least I'm not advocating all sorts of sexual perversions like you and Dr. Jones."

HIM: (Shouting even louder.) "I called you to have a Christian-to-Christian discussion. Are you trying to make fun of me?"

ME: "No, I'm trying to keep from crying over you."

HIM: "That does it. I don't have to take this!" (He slams down the receiver.)

Later the next week, on my way to work one morning, my car was hit in the rear by an older man who claimed that he was eating a banana and didn't see the light turn red. This seemed a reasonable explanation for why he crushed my bumper. We exchanged business cards. His card listed him as a professor of evangelism at Bob Jones University. It had a scripture quotation on the back of the card along with the slogan "Witnessing Is My Business."

For the time being I have sworn off having fun with the folk at Bob Jones. No more late night phone calls for me. They play rough. Not that they scare me, but I have a wife and two children to think about.

6

*Religious satirical verse has a rich and many-sided history,
as this brief survey of religious humorous poetry shows.
Sometimes the sharpest wit comes in rhyme.*

RELIGION IN RHYME

"The Bishop's Last Directions"

Tell my priests, when I am gone,
    O'er me to shed no tears,
For I shall be no deader then
    Than they have been for years.

—Unknown

"Religion"

Those petulant capricious sects,
The maggots of corrupted texts . . .

—Samuel Butler

"The Religion of Hudibras"

For his religion it was fit
To match his learning and his wit:
'Twas Presbyterian true blue;
For he was of that stubborn crew
Of errant saints, whom all men grant
To be the true church militant;
Such as do build their faith upon
The holy text of pike and gun;

Decide all controversies by
Infallible artillery;
And prove their doctrine orthodox,
By apostolic blows and knocks;
Call fire, and sword, and desolation,
A godly, thorough reformation,
Which always must be carried on,
And still be doing, never done;
As if religion were intended
For nothing else but to be mended:
A sect whose chief devotion lies
In odd perverse antipathies;
In falling out with that or this,
And finding somewhat still amiss;
More peevish, cross, and splenetic,
Than dog distract, or monkey sick;
That with more care keep holy-day
The wrong, than others the right way,
Compound for sins they are inclin'd to,
By damning those they have no mind to:
Still so perverse and opposite,
As if they worshipped God for spite:
The self-same thing they will abhor
One way, and long another for:
Free-will they one way disavow,
Another, nothing else allow:
All piety consists therein
In them, in other men all sin:
Rather than fail, they will defy
That which they love most tenderly;
Quarrel with minc'd pies and disparage
Their best and dearest friend, plum porridge,
Fat pig and goose itself oppose,
And blaspheme custard through the nose.

—Samuel Butler

"Predestination"

We are the precious chosen few:
Let all the rest be damned.
There's only room for one or two:
We can't have heaven crammed.

    —Unknown

"Untitled"

The church and clergy here, no doubt,
Are very much akin;
Both weather-beaten are without,
Both empty are within.

    —Jonathan Swift

"Untitled"

By plain analogy we're told
Why first the church was called the fold:
Into the fold the sheep are steered
There guarded from the wolf and—sheared.

    —Ambrose Bierce

(Bierce elsewhere defines "clergyman" as "a man who undertakes the management of our spiritual affairs as a method of bettering his temporal ones.")

"The Village Choir"

(After the Charge of the Light Brigade)

Half a bar, half a bar,
Half a bar onward!
Into an awful ditch
Choir and precentor hitch,

Into a mess of pitch,
They led the Old Hundred.
Trebles to right of them,
Tenors to left of them,
Basses in front of them,
Bellowed and thundered.
Oh, that precentor's look,
When the sopranos took
Their own time and hook
From the Old Hundred!

Screeched all the trebles here,
Boggled the tenors there,
Raising the parson's hair,
While his mind wandered;
Theirs not to reason why
This psalm was pitched too high:
Theirs but to gasp and cry
Out the Old Hundred.
Trebles to right of them,
Tenors to left of them;
Basses in front of them,
Bellowed and thundered.
Stormed they with shout and yell,
Not wise they sang nor well,
Drowning the sexton's bell,
While all the church wondered.

Dire the precentor's glare,
Flashed his pitchfork in air,
Sounding fresh keys to bear
Out of Old Hundred.
Swiftly he turned his back,
Reached he his hat from rack,
Then from the screaming pack,
Himself he sundered.
Trebles to right of him,
Tenors to left of him,

Discords behind him
Bellowed and thundered.
Oh, the wild howls they wrought:
Right to the end they fought!
Some tune they sang, but not,
Not the Old Hundred.

—Anonymous

"A Short Sermon"

(Delivered in usual singsong style of the conventional curate.)

I am going to preach to you this morning, my friends, upon
the young man who was sick of the palsy. Now, this young
man was sick of the palsy. Now, this young man was sick of the
palsy. The palsy, as you are well aware, is a very terrible
disease, a wasting scourge. And this young man was sick of the
palsy. And the palsy, as you know, is strongly hereditary. It
had been in his family. His father had been sick of the palsy,
and his mother had been sick of the palsy, and they had all of
them, in fact, been sick of the palsy. And this young man had
been sick of the palsy. Yes, my dear friends, he had had it for
years and years, and—he was sick of it.

—Anonymous

7

The Convention *is Baptist prophet Will D. Campbell's account of the 1994 convention of the Federal Baptist Church, mythical successor to the Southern Baptist Convention. In Campbell's modern parable, we follow a Mississippi Baptist couple, Exell and Dorcas Rose McBride, to the convention where, through a strange turn of events, Dorcas Rose will be nominated and elected as the first female president of the Federal Baptists. In the first excerpt, Exell attends a meeting of a group of liberated Baptist men who are busy rediscovering the masculine "Christ beast within." Campbell, who has said that he "does not care for feminist, male, black, liberation or any other adjective linked to the word 'theology,'" appears to be making fun of adjectival theology.*

In the second excerpt, Campbell leads us through the rollicking opening ceremonies of the convention in which, as sometimes happens in church circles, there appears to be more style than substance. Campbell has served as Baptist pastor, university chaplain, civil rights leader, and farmer. Now, from his small farm in middle Tennessee, he ministers to the rich and the poor, the famous and the infamous—and serves as ever-present gadfly in his books, such as The Convention.

SELECTIONS FROM
*THE CONVENTION**

Will D. Campbell

"THE CONVENTION BEGINS"

The Stevenson Expressway was stalled all the way to Dan Ryan, and cab drivers honked impatiently while their vehicles crawled along Kennedy Expressway. Two full-sized church buses had sideswiped each other, so traffic was backed up almost to O'Hare Airport. Chicago was buzzing with Baptists. Commissioners were streaming into the city from every direction as the 1994 Convention of the Federal Baptist Church was about to begin. The area around McCormick Place on the Lake, one of the largest convention centers in America, was jammed with motor homes and buses. And on most were signs, banners, and bumper stickers bearing such slogans as "Chicago or Bust," "God's Wheels," "Warner Robbins Has the Air Force and First Baptist," "Alabama Is God's Country," "Alaska Baptists Are Not Cold," and "We Brake for Baptists."

By the time Exell and Dorcas McBride reached downtown Chicago, they were weary. Over the years they had traveled very little. When Volene was thirteen, they had taken her to Daytona Beach and had rented a furnished apartment. Later, when Volene was in college, they had stayed in small motels a few times when visiting their daughter. But none of that had prepared them for the Ruthenbeck Hotel.

"I think I'd better park it," Exell told the doorman after the uniformed hotel employee had directed bellmen to unload the McBrides' luggage, then had handed Exell a garage check and asked the guest to leave the keys in his Saturn sedan. ". . . Sometimes it's kind of stubborn," Exell added, even though the doorman had already gone to the next car waiting in line.

The doorman looked sideways, winked at the waiting driver of a sleek Porsche and mumbled to the parking attendant, "Hicksville Ferry. Check the trunk for live chickens," then he smiled politely as he turned back to Exell and said, "Oh, we drive all kinds, sir."

Exell shrugged and watched as the driver slid into the McBrides' car and whisked the vehicle into the garage entrance. "Now just how am I going to know where he parked it?" Exell asked Dorcas, who shook her head and walked stiffly toward the entrance to the hotel lobby.

Inside, the hotel clerk had trouble finding their reservations on the computer.

"Brother Sutton called it in way last winter," Dorcas told the woman.

"Who?" the woman asked. "Is *Brother* his first name?"

Exell motioned to Dorcas that they should go someplace else, but she gave him the look that meant "Be patient." He sighed, and she carefully explained to the clerk that their minister, a "brother in Christ," was named Byron Sutton and that the reservation might be listed under his name, though he did not want to be called "Reverend," which is why she called him "Brother." The clerk appeared agitated but soon found the reservation under Sutton's name.

After they had been shown to their room by a bellhop and had unpacked, Dorcas reminded Exell that their pastor had told them the first thing they should do was to find the convention center and register as commissioners. So they strolled along the walkway from the hotel to the convention center. Along the way they were accosted by dozens of interest-group representatives who were passing out leaflets, selling souvenirs and lobbying for causes and candidates.

Several women, and two men wearing clerical collars, walked back and forth carying picket signs on which had been imprinted: "A WOMAN'S GOD-GIVEN BODY IS HER OWN—FREE CHOICE." An equal number of opposing picketers tried to walk in step beside the others. On the countering signs had been imprinted the slogan: "ALL BODIES, BIG AND SMALL, BELONG TO GOD—THOU SHALT NOT KILL." Occasionally, one or another of the protestors would bump into an opposing picketer, forcing the other off the main walkway and into the planters which lined the walkway's glass shield.

At the walkway's entrance into the convention center, a small booth had been set up under a sign: "NORTH AMERICAN BAPTIST PEACE FELLOWSHIP." Those around it tried to engage passersby in conversation. Anyone who slowed down but didn't stop was handed pamphlets bearing the headline, "MUST WE RAPE MEXICO AGAIN?" Adjacent to this booth was another, fashioned like a wigwam. "AMERICA: CHOSEN OF GOD" was written in crude, backwoods scrawl on the tent flap. Several men and women wearing Puritan hats milled about the area and handed out pamphlets calling for a strong national defense.

Dorcas took whatever was handed her and placed it in her purse. Exell simply shook his head, no, at whoever approached him. Once they entered the cavernous display area inside McCormick Place on the Lake, Exell and Dorcas held hands and walked close to one another, as if they were walking on a strange planet, encountering thousands of alien creatures and looking desperately for someone like themselves.

* * *

Inside the convention center that evening, a choir of five-year-old children was singing at the closing session of the Home Mission Conference:

> Welcome to the open door.
> None too weary, none too poor.
> Reaching out from shore to shore,
> 'A Million More in Ninety-four.'

Each child was dressed in a different ethnic or national costume. Swiss children in leather breeches, Dutch with wooden shoes, Latinos with sombreros. There was an Appalachian boy with coal dust on his face, and a black child from Alabama who wore faded overalls and no shoes.

The thousands who had gathered in the convention center roared their approval. The director of the choir, a very obese woman of about sixty, bowed to the crowd then led the children in the lilting refrain:

> Eight, nine, ten and more;
> 'A Million More in Ninety-four.'

On cue, the children began to exit the stage, but the audience would not let them go. The director motioned for the choir to come back. The confused and frightened children bumped into each other as some turned one way and some another. When they were back in place, however, they sang the jingle again, their callow voices bending under the strain of high notes:

> Welcome to the open door,
> None too weary, none too poor.
> Reaching out from shore to shore,
> 'A Million More in Ninety-four.'

And they screamed the counting in the refrain, their director's baton egging them on:

> Eight, nine, ten and more;
> 'A Million More in Ninety-four.'

Two years earlier Dr. Harry Epperson, the church's executive secretary, had told Senator John Morris Purdue that membership in the new church was not rising as they had projected when the Southern Baptist Convention had become the Federal Baptist Church. The senator, a leader in the recently reorganized Federal Baptist Church, recommended that the church employ the Eric Bullington public-relations firm to conduct a policy and strategy seminar. The seminar cost the church one hundred thousand dollars. Purdue said it was worth the money. "A good slogan is hard to come by." And the slogan they produced was "A Million More in Ninety-four." Ironically, neither of them knew that the same slogan had been used forty years earlier, and only the year had been changed.

Armed with this, and in order to meet the desired quota, the senator then devised a plan to start mission congregations in ethnic neighborhoods and communities across the country.

A few black congregations had already affiliated with the Federal Baptist Church. In some areas where demographics changed rapidly, in-coming black people were joining existing white congregations. Some suspected that the senator had a sinister motive in his scheme: to keep blacks and certain other minorities out of previously all-white churches, because with a strong church as the backbone of an ethnic neighborhood, it would remain separate and ethnic.

Whatever the senator's reason, the program was proving successful. A hundred million dollars had been appropriated for the Home Mission Board to use in starting new churches, and the goal was well on its way. At an evangelism conference in Louisiana, which established a large number of the mission churches, Purdue had meant to report on the prorated cost of each soul saved, but instead he said, "A hundred dollars a head is a small price to pay." Now Purdue and Epperson were backstage, watching their plan in action on closed-circuit television. When the children were off the stage, a dapper young preacher was introduced as minister of puppetry at Royal Arms Baptist Church in Washington, D.C. He ran to the center of the footlights and held a ventriloquist's Oriental dummy. The doll recited some scripture passages and sang "Jesus Loves Me" while the man drank a glass of water. Then the doll gave his testimony on how he got saved at a Baptist Vacation Bible School. The audience's responses seemed divided between approval and disgust.

Then the minister of puppetry called one by one the choir children back on stage, and the doll asked each child what the church had done for him or her. Most gave the same answer: "Told me about Jesus." The preacher seemed to want a different response, so he singled out a little black girl wearing a plain gingham dress and a red ribbon in her peppercorn hair. He placed the doll on the floor and took the child in his lap. Her full rounded lips were pink, and her nose dripped from a head cold.

"What? No watermelon?" said a woman seated toward the middle of the audience.

"Shushhhh," someone said.

"And what did you learn in VBS?" the ventriloquist's doll called up from the floor.

The little girl leaned over and looked down at it. "Dey tole me 'bout Christmas."

Somewhat daunted, the young man spoke in his own voice. "Oh. You mean they told you about Christ. About Jesus. Don't you?"

"Nosuh. Dey tole us 'bout Christmas."

"And what did they tell you?" he asked, fidgeting in his chair. "Uh . . . What is Christmas?"

A mucus bubble from the girl's nostril broke as she was speaking: "Datst wen de angels come down and bees widju fo' a lil' wile. And den dey goes back up."

"This is criminal," the same woman said, but louder than before. "Why doesn't the idiot give her a Kleenex instead of parading her in his circus?"

"Hush, Lilith," her friend whispered.

The young preacher held the girl away from his body as he put her down. "Uh, well. That's cute," he said.

The children's program was followed by a giant extravaganza from the ethnic mission congregations. "Give them a big celebration," the senator had told Epperson. "Recognize them in some special way. They love pageantry. Send them home happy, and they'll bring a friend next time." Epperson had also arranged for the senator to address the gathering first. Purdue talked for thirty minutes about Americans being a chosen people, about the evils of communism and the need for a strong military to ensure that Biblical prophecy will come to pass. He was followed by the president of the Home Mission Board—also handpicked by Purdue at the formation of the Federal Baptist Church—who preached on the "Great Commission."

At the conclusion of his sermon, three thousand members of the new ethnic congregations gathered on the massive stage built for the occasion. Like the children, these adults had been told to dress in national and ethnic costumes. Many of them were so embellished, imagined and exaggerated, that they looked more like costumes for a Halloween ball or a Mardi Gras parade than a Home Mission demonstration. Indian chieftains with full feather headdresses, and others in Polynesian muumuus, Japanese kimonos, Pakistani saris, but also tunics, doublets, togas, caftans and calpacs. There were African warriors, Japanese dancers, fat women in Victorian gowns, Lapp herders, Spanish bullfighters, Russian ballerinas, and grease-painted South Sea islanders. They came in single file from the wings of the stage, in no particular order, the colors clashing, the costumes mingling into a hodgepodge of unpurposed brandishment.

The procession took longer than expected, longer even than their performance. What they did was recite the "Great Commission" text in unison, all in their native tongues. The sound was more cacophonous than pentecostal, though occasionally an English voice could be understood to say:

> Go ye therefore, and teach all nations, baptizing them in the name of the Father, and of the Son, and of the Holy Ghost: Teaching them to observe all things whatsoever I have commanded you: and, lo, I am with you always, even unto the end of the world.

"THE CHRISTIAN MEN'S MOVEMENT"

"You're a bull elephant, barreling through the jungle. Nothing can stop you," yelled the leader on the platform when Exell McBride entered the conference hall after the morning workshop had begun. "You can uproot trees. Storms and cannons don't stop you. Lions and tigers? Poo! A petty nuisance," the man continued. Exell looked a second time at the sign on the door to make certain he was in the right place. "Bellow!" the man yelled louder. "Lift your trunks and sound the warning: the elephant is coming, the elephant is coming!" Exell, embarrassed at being late, looked quickly for a seat.

"Nothing stops a bull elephant!" the man screamed, pausing for breath. He was big, heavy, dressed in black. As he moved about the platform, he was a sight of hair and leather, fashioned for a Harley.

Exell found a seat near the middle of the large room just as a soft, timid voice near him responded, "Nothing but a cow elephant."

"Who said that?" the man at the microphone snapped. "We are here to set ourselves free from the force field of women. Only a man in prison would say that. I want the one who said that to come forward. Luke, four: eighteen."

As he sat, Exell regretted having come. He was there by accident. Earlier, when he had walked with Dorcas to the hotel to have coffee with some women she had met at the Monday evening conference for women, someone had handed him a flyer announcing this meeting: "ATTEND THE CHRISTIAN MEN'S MOVEMENT—A seminar on searching for the Christ beast within you. Be all that you can be. BE A MAN!"

Exell had intended to throw the flyer in a trash can, but Dorcas had said, "You should go. I met a lot of nice women at my workshop. Maybe you'll make some new friends."

Exell had responded that he just wanted to meet somebody here besides her "who has some sense." Seated in this conference, however, Exell wondered if he would.

The leader was prancing from one end of the platform to the other, coming to the very edge, shading his eyes from the light and peering into the audience to identify the one who had spoken. The leader was visibly agitated, face red, veins standing out on his neck like mole runs on a well-kept lawn. "Liberty to the captives. Release to those in prison. That's what Jesus said he came for."

For a moment, irritation overcame the leader and he stood silent, mopping his brow. Then he flounced the length of the stage again, yelling, "Do you want to be set free? Do you believe in *Jeee-sus?*" He whispered the name, repeating it over and over in the same sanctimonious fashion. He was trying to sound like all the evangelists he had ever heard trying to sound like all the others they had heard before them.

"Blessed be the name. Release to prisoners. Delivery to captives," the man said as he twirled the long microphone cord like a lariat and bowed his fat legs so that he walked like a cowboy with heavy chaps. "Jesus. Jeee-sus. Jeee-sus! He came to set us free."

Exell no more knew what to make of what he was watching than he had of most that he had seen since they had arrived. He tried to understand, to appropriate what was going on around him. But the trying was like struggling to walk through deep Mississippi mud with heavy boots. What he saw was as strange to him as fish walking on land. He felt neither inferior nor defective. Not even confused. Just removed from it all. The way he had felt the day his grandfather died, asking for a book to hold in his hands. Exell remembered wondering that day why his grandfather held a book he couldn't read, yet sure that his grandfather knew more than the book contained.

Before Exell had entered the conference hall, the man on the platform had been introduced as "the facilitator." As such, he had intoned the name of Jesus while a choir of twenty-five barrel-chested men, standing to the left of the stage, had begun a stentorious bellow in unison. They were stripped from the waist up, their pants the same black as the facilitator's. With their heads thrown back until their faces paralleled the ceiling, the choir had been trying to make the sounds of an elephant herd just as Exell had taken a wrong turn in the corridor before circling around to enter this conference hall. What had come out from the choir's attempts at elephant sounds was more a combination of coyote howls and donkey brays. With their heavy and hairy chests heaving, bellies lapping over their wide belts with silver-plated buckles which had been embossed with the thin outline of a fish bearing the Greek letters ΙΧΘΥΣ, they appeared to be a chorus in a comic opera.

Doops Momber was covering the Christian Men's Movement workshop with television equipment. All of the carrying cases and cameras carried his logo, a purple hyena superimposed on a white spire, and the large lettering, *SMM, Inc.*

He had previously contracted with several independent stations to do a half-hour show called "Highlights and Sidelights." As Doops watched this spectacle, it crossed his mind that he might have something one of the networks would go for.

He had two VCR cameras in operation. One was fixed on a tripod far to the side of the seminar participants. The other was a hand unit he used for close-up and action shots. Just before Exell had entered the hall, Doops had stepped in front of the stationary camera as commentator. As he spoke on camera, he glanced occasionally at a manuscript he had prepared:

> The Christian Men's Movement which evolved out of the New Men's Movement of the Eighties, a nonreligious order seeking restoration of lost masculinity, was gurued by a famous poet, Robert Bly.
>
> At first it was largely confined to places like Cambridge and Berkeley and consisted of male academics who had been sympathizers and fellow travelers with the Feminist Movement. Together they had carried picket signs, assisted in ridding books, stories, old picture shows and children's classics of sexist language and attempted to prove, at least to their own satisfaction, that they were as liberal back home in the academy as they had been, years before, on the Selma March or in resisting the Vietnam War with the Rev. William Sloan Coffin. . . .

While Doops spoke to the camera, the participants had served as an animated backdrop. The choir had resumed their elephant sounds, but in subdued tones. The low bellowing was to the tune of "Just As I Am" while the facilitator persisted in his harangue. Because the choir members had their eyes closed and because they were not getting enough oxygen, the men's bodies were off balance, swaying to and fro, side to side, sometimes bumping into each other, scrambling for equilibrium as they did.

When Doops went back to the portable camera, the facilitator was still beseeching the erring one who had said, "Nothing but a cow elephant."

A man carrying a crossbow stood. He was the guilty one, and he responded to the facilitator's invitation to come forward. Doops zoomed the camera lens to a full-faced shot of the man's sheepish grin as he eased past the row of men, including Exell, then made his way down the aisle and past men who had moved from their chairs and were sitting in the lotus position. Each clutched his "power object," which he had been instructed to bring "to suggest inner strength." The power objects ranged from Bibles to Skoal cans, golf clubs to a paper bag filled with EverReady flashlight batteries.

As the transgressor approached the platform, the facilitator moved down the steps to meet him at floor level. The choir stopped abruptly in the middle of a bar, and the choirmaster turned to face the audience. He flexed and waggled his right arm in the air the way a jubilant elephant might do his trunk, then he let out a short, piercing shrill. The choir echoed in unison.

The man with the crossbow moved toward the facilitator, as if to offer a fraternal embrace. The facilitator gave him a clamping handshake instead. The man then handed the facilitator the medieval contraption, which he accepted with cautious hesitation. The small winch that cocked the steel bow was wound tight. There was no quarrel—standard ammunition for the weapon—in the guilding slot, but as the facilitator examined it, moving the weapon in different directions, some of the men on the front rows scurried for cover. Maybe recalling stories of the crossbow's armor-piercing range of three hundred yards, or remembering that several popes had banned its use (except against infidels) because of its atrocity.

Doops moved back to the fixed camera and began his commentary again:

. . . The New Men's Movement had begun when the Cambridge and Berkeley sympathizers realized that those they had deigned to help, to lift from the swamp of oppression—oppression designed by a system of which they

were sure they were not a part—were not talking of equal pay
for equal work in the marketplace of plebian skills.

In fact, these women were talking of administrative and
curricula control, the same control the men had, before and
now; instructors becoming deans and chancellors, as the men
had been, and they were still. . . .

Doops paused and leaned forward, knowing that his
closeness to the camera would produce an out-of-focus,
confused frame. His dark, beady eyes probed the depth of the
camera lens as he continued, his tone sardonic:

> . . . What do they want now?
> Because I don't have a uterus, I'm no longer
> welcome in the faculty lounge. . . .

"What do you do to feed and clothe your cave?" the
facilitator asked the transgressor who stood before him.
"What kind of work do you do?"

"We run an alligator farm in southern Florida—"

"We," the facilitator said. Not as a question. "Then I take it
you have a woman. Any young?"

"Three. Pretty much grown, though." The man stood at a
rigid military parade rest position, feet spread, hands clasped
behind his back.

"And your woman. She boss you around?"

"Sometimes."

"Why?"

The man didn't respond. Just looked at the facilitator the
way he might have if he had been asked what planet they were
on.

"You have a lawn in front of your cave?"

"Oh, we don't have a cave. We have a house. Spanish
ranch-style. Four bedrooms. Combination kitchen/dining
room. Big den, too. No fireplace, though. Don't need a
fireplace in Florida. Aw, once in a blue moon you might, but
we don't have one." The man's tone was not one of offense.
More like answering the questions of a confused child. "Had

two in our house in Virginia. But had central heat. Never used the fireplaces. Hardly ever."

"In the movement we call it a 'cave,'" the facilitator said, his voice crusted with cultivated roughness, making it clear that the man's staccato voice had been as annoying to the leader as the man's words. "Who cuts the grass?"

"My wife does all that. I don't like to mow the lawn. To cut stuff down. I'd just let it grow. That's what my wife says. Says I'd 'let it grow 'til it looked like we were living in a wilderness.'"

"Good, good, GOOD!" the facilitator cheered. "That's the beast within us as plain as day." The choir roared as the audience applauded. "You'd rather live in a jungle. Kill alligators with a spear. Good—"

"We don't kill the alligators," the man said softly, but the facilitator persisted.

"—But your woman is trying to tame you. Domesticate you. Roar, brother. Stand tall! BE A MAN. Spear those gators. Drag them through the jungle and throw them at her feet to skin. Good, good, good!" He handed the crossbow back to the man and looked around for someone else to respond.

"We breed the gators," the man said, now standing at ease. "Sell the fingerlings to tourists as souvenirs. Actually, they aren't alligators. They're crocodiles and cute as a button. Them little boogers—"

The facilitator waved the man back toward his seat, but the man ignored him. "You see, we're both retired. Raising gators is more of a hobby than anything else. We make some money at it, but it's really more of a hobby. My wife flew for American Airlines. Flew for some big companies before that. She went to the Air Force Academy. Pilots retire young, you know. And I was a CPA. Folks called me a bean counter, but we didn't care. I didn't anyway, and she said she didn't either. I was too young to quit when she did, but I retired anyway."

Doops was having such a hard time not laughing out loud that he walked over to the far camera and pretended to get some distance and angle shots as the man continued: "Both of us made good money. Most of the time I made almost as much as she did. Then we moved to Florida from northern Virginia. I couldn't stand the cold winter so we moved to Florida. I was always sickly. Even as a kid. Had a lot of colds and flu and stuff. Even after I had my adenoids out. Had asthma too. Don't now. My wife used to say that was mostly on account of my nerves. Nothing like a boar alligator to calm a fellow's nerves. Hahahahaha."

The facilitator, standing with his hands on his hips, did not laugh. He glowered down at the man, who seemed puzzled but also more nervous. The man increased his tempo as he went on speaking, "My wife started collecting these things." He pulled the trigger of the crossbow and let the steel bow give a deep thwaching sound, like the lowest note of a bass drum. There was a scattered tittering around the room. "She brought the first one back from Italy. She used to fly from New York to Rome. It was made over eight hundred years ago. Though this isn't that one. She won't let me carry that one. Says I might lose it. This one was made around Nineteen-fifty. Used for deer hunting. Not by me though. I don't hunt. Aw, I'd kill a rabbit or something if I had to, but I never was much of a hunter. We just collect crossbows. Got twenty-four of them in all."

When the facilitator stepped forward, trying to halt the unwanted testimony, the speaker rushed on. In rapid bursts. "Some folks say our crossbows are worth a fortune. My wife says they're disaster insurance. Never know. This day and time. She told me to bring this one. When I told her I was supposed to bring a power object. Fact is, she told me about the seminar. I do declare if I don't believe that woman—"

The facilitator interrupted, booming into the microphone. "Thank you. Mister? I don't think I caught your name, but never mind. That's a nice power object, but we have to share some others."

The man, holding the crossbow high above his head to keep from hitting anyone, returned to his row and sidled along it to his seat. During the lull, Doops took his place again as commentator in front of the camera:

> . . . What those men saw as a massacre in the academy spread beyond, and soon the New Men's Movement went on to include doctors, lawyers, Army officers, accountants and dozer operators, ordinary men of every ilk.
>
> Today they pay high fees to join the movement and spend numerous weekends attending seminars and conferences on regaining lost masculinity.
>
> It has even spread to the strongest bastion of things as they were, and perhaps ought to stay—the Christian Men's Movement—with a new chapter in the Federal Baptist Church: "searching for the Christ beast within."

All the while, Exell had been watching. Trying to sort it all out. He had thought of tree frogs singing in tall timbers, warning him of rain that he neither dreaded nor welcomed but would simply accept as the work of the Lord.

Suddenly someone yelled from the center of the crowd, "I hear the women's caucus is going to run a woman for president." "President of what?" a voice yelled from the rear of the hall. "President of the FBC."

"Now *that's* funny," one of the shirtless men in the choir responded. It gave everyone the occasion to laugh that they had been wanting since the timid alligator farmer had gone to the front. Everyone except Exell. He didn't laugh, and something about their laughter offended him. He wasn't sure what it was and didn't dwell on it. But for a moment it bothered him. He knew it was supposed to be funny—the thought of a woman trying to be president of something as big as the Federal Baptist Church. He didn't remember ever thinking about that being a possibility. But in that moment, Exell didn't remember ever thinking about it not being a possibility either. He felt strange.

The facilitator, annoyed at the droll interlude which had thrown his workshop off course, struggled to regain the leadership. As the men laughed, he held his right hand up for silence. "No, no, no," he said, his smile more of a frown. "No politics in here. That's not what I'm here for. The movement paid me to . . . I mean, the administration of this convention. That was one of the conditions . . . I'm not supposed to . . . don't know anything about what's happening in your church. I'm not even a Baptist." As soon as those words slipped from his mouth, the facilitator stopped himself. "I mean, I am a Christian just like the rest of you. But they said I . . . we . . . are not to get into politics. I know Baptists aren't political when it comes to their church—not that Presbyterians are, either."

The choirmaster, trained or intuiting, led his glee club to an upbeat elephant rendition of "Onward Christian Soldiers." As the choir bellowed, the facilitator pretended to be in deep meditation. When they stopped, he began encouraging different men to stand and tell boyhood experiences. Some talked of fathers they seldom saw, of domineering mothers, wives or sisters. As each man spoke, he clutched his power object. The facilitator or one of his aides interpreted the symbols. Some, they said, were of hope. Some of discord. Some of utter helplessness. The men were assured that all could be useful in setting loose "the wild man within" and breaking out of the "force field of women."

Then the workshop broke into smaller groups where the men sat cross-legged in circles on the floor and wrote deep secret fears on pieces of paper. They threw what they had written into flaming bedpans which the facilitator had placed in the middle of each circle. Next, the men drew pictures or scribbled horrid images on newsprint. The facilitator's assistants explained what each drawing meant and helped the men analyze and explain what they had created.

Exell, who at first had silently but sternly refused to participate in any of the exercises, finally drew a tiny stick man on a large horse. Nearby, he drew a huge man standing in front of a mansion-like dwelling.

An assistant to the facilitator, after asking Exell where he had been born and being told Texas, explained that Exell probably harbored a deep resentment that those who do the work on ranches are called cow*boys*, while those who own the ranches are called cattle*men*. Then the assistant told Exell that was off the subject and that Exell should try again.

Exell thanked him politely, told the assistant he was thinking of Dale Alan, his foster son back home, when he had drawn the picture. Exell also said he didn't think he better stay for the rest of the occasion because he really didn't understand what they were driving at.

The assistant asked if Exell would share his power object before he left.

Exell fished in his shirt pocket and found a toothpick, which he had made from a goose quill. He held it up for the group to see, then turned and left the building.

8

The diminutive Owen Meany is the subject of John Irving's best-selling novel A Prayer for Owen Meany. *Who is little Owen and what does he represent? Many readers of the novel believe that he is the Christ-figure, an incarnation of the presence of a God who came in weakness, strangeness, taking the form of human flesh. If indeed Owen functions figuratively in this way, then that makes all the more interesting—and funny—his descriptions of the bilateral religious establishment in his New England town.*

Congregationalists or Episcopalians, preachers or their spouses—under the gaze of John Irving, all are fit subjects for holy humor.

SELECTION FROM
*A PRAYER FOR OWEN MEANY**

John Irving

There were also vast differences between the Rev. Lewis Merrill, whom I liked, and the Rev. Dudley Wiggin—the rector of the Episcopal Church—who was a bumpkin of boredom.

To compare these two ministers as dismissively as I did, I confess I was drawing on no small amount of snobbery inherited from Grandmother Wheelwright. The Congregationalists had *pastors*—the Rev. Lewis Merrill was our pastor. If you grow up with that comforting word, it's hard to accept *rectors*—the Episcopal Church had rectors; the Rev. Dudley Wiggin was the rector of Christ Church, Gravesend. I shared

*From *A Prayer for Owen Meany* by John Irving. Copyright © 1989 by John Irving. Used with permission of William Morrow & Co, Inc.

my grandmother's distaste for the word *rector*—it sounded too much like *rectum* to be taken seriously.

But it would have been hard to take the Rev. Dudley Wiggin seriously if he'd been a pastor. Whereas the Rev. Mr. Merrill had heeded his calling as a young man—he had always been in, and of, the church—the Rev. Mr. Wiggin was a former airline pilot; some difficulty with his eyesight had forced his early retirement from the skies, and he had descended to our wary town with a newfound fervor—the zeal of the convert giving him the healthy but frantic appearance of one of those "elder" citizens who persist in entering vigorous sporting competitions in the over-fifty category. Whereas Pastor Merrill spoke an educated language—he'd been an English major at Princeton; he'd heard Niebuhr and Tillich lecture at Union Theological— *Rector* Wiggin spoke in ex-pilot homilies; he was a pulpit-thumper who had no doubt.

What made Mr. Merrill infinitely more attractive was that he was *full* of doubt; he expressed *our* doubt in the most eloquent and sympathetic ways. In his completely lucid and convincing view, the Bible is a book with a troubling plot, but a plot that can be understood: God creates us out of love, but we don't want God, or we don't believe in Him, or we pay very poor attention to Him. Nevertheless, God continues to love us—at least, He continues to try to get our attention. Pastor Merrill made religion seem *reasonable*. And the trick of having faith, he said, was that it was necessary to believe in God *without* any great or even remotely reassuring evidence that we don't inhabit a godless universe.

Although he knew all the best—or, at least, the least boring—stories in the Bible, Mr. Merrill was most appealing because he reassured us that doubt was the essence of faith, and not faith's opposite. By comparison, whatever the Rev. Dudley Wiggin had seen to make him believe in God, he had seen absolutely—possibly by flying an airplane too close to the sun. The rector was *not* gifted with language, and he was blind to doubt or worry in any form; perhaps the problem with his "eyesight" that had forced his early retirement from the airlines was really a euphemism for the blinding power of his total religious conversion—because Mr. Wiggin was fearless to an extent that would have made him an unsafe pilot, and to an extent that made him a madman as a preacher.

Even his Bible selections were outlandish; a satirist could not have selected them better. The Rev. Mr. Wiggin was especially fond of the word "firmament"; there was always a firmament in his Bible selections. And he loved all allusions to faith as a *battle* to be savagely fought and won; faith was a war waged against faith's *adversaries*. "Take the whole armor of God!" he would rave. We were instructed to wear "the breastplate of righteousness"; our faith was a "shield"— against "all the flaming darts of the evil one." The rector said he wore a "helmet of salvation." That's from Ephesians; Mr. Wiggin was a big fan of Ephesians. He also whooped it up about Isaiah—especially the part when "the Lord is sitting upon a throne"; the rector was big on the Lord upon a throne. The Lord is surrounded by seraphim. One of the seraphim flies to Isaiah, who is complaining that he's "a man of unclean lips." Not for long; not according to Isaiah. The seraphim touches Isaiah's mouth with "a burning coal" and Isaiah is as good as new.

That was what we heard from the Rev. Dudley Wiggin: all the unlikeliest miracles.

"I DON'T LIKE THE SERAPHIM," Owen complained. "WHAT'S THE POINT OF BEING SCARY?"

But although Owen agreed with me that the rector was a moron who messed up the Bible for tentative believers by assaulting us with the worst of God the Almighty and God the Terrible—and although Owen acknowledged that the Rev. Mr. Wiggin's sermons were about as entertaining and convincing as a pilot's voice in the intercom, explaining technical difficulties while the plane plummets toward the earth and the stewardesses are screaming—Owen actually preferred Wiggin to what little he knew of Pastor Merrill. Owen didn't know much about Mr. Merrill, I should add;

Owen was never a Congregationalist. But Merrill was *such* a popular preacher that parishioners from the other Gravesend churches would frequently skip a service of their own to attend his sermons. Owen did so, on occasion, but Owen was always critical. Even when Gravesend Academy bestowed the intellectual honor upon Pastor Merill—of inviting him to be a frequent guest preacher in the academy's nondenominational church—Owen was critical.

"BELIEF IS NOT AN INTELLECTUAL MATTER," he complained. "IF HE'S GOT SO MUCH DOUBT, HE'S IN THE WRONG BUSINESS."

But who, besides Owen Meany and Rector Wiggin, had so *little* doubt? Owen was a natural in the belief business, but my appreciation of Mr. Merrill and my contempt for Mr. Wiggin were based on common sense. I took a particularly Yankee view of them; the Wheelwright in me was all in favor of Lewis Merrill, all opposed to Dudley Wiggin. We Wheelwrights do not scoff at the appearance of things. Things often *are* as they appear. First impressions matter. That clean, well-lit place of worship, which was the Congregational Church—its pristine white clapboards, its tall, clear windows that welcomed the view of branches against the sky—that was a first impression that lasted for me; it was a model of purity and no-nonsense, against which the Episcopal gloom of stone and tapestry and stained glass could pose no serious competition. And Pastor Merrill was also good-looking—in an intense, pale, slightly undernourished way. He had a boyish face—a sudden, winning, embarrassed smile that contradicted a fairly constant look of worry that more usually gave him the expression of an anxious child. An errant lock of hair flopped on his forehead when he looked down upon his sermon, or bent over his Bible—his hair problem was the unruly result of a pronounced widow's peak, which further contributed to his boyishness. And he was always misplacing his glasses, which he didn't seem to need—that is, he could read without them, he could look out upon his congregation without them (at least not appearing to be blind); then, all of a sudden, he would commence a frantic search for them. It was endearing; so was his slight stutter, because it made us nervous for him—afraid for him, should he have his eloquence snatched from him and be struck down with a crippling speech impediment. He was articulate, but he never made speech seem effortless; on the contrary, he exhibited what hard work it was—to make his faith, in tandem with his doubt, clear; to speak well, in spite of his stutter.

And then, to add to Mr. Merrill's appeal, we pitied him for his family. His wife was from California, the sunny part. My grandmother used to speculate that she had been one of those permanently tanned, bouncy blondes—a perfectly whole-some type, but entirely too easily persuaded that good health and boundless energy for good deeds were the natural results of clean living and practical values. No one had told her that health and energy and the Lord's work are harder to come by in bad weather. Mrs. Merrill suffered in New Hampshire.

She suffered visibly. Her blondness turned to dry straw; her cheeks and nose turned a raw salmon color, her eyes watered—she caught every flu, every common cold there was; no epidemic missed her. Aghast at the loss of her California color, she tried makeup; but this turned her skin to clay. Even in summer, she couldn't tan; she turned so dead white in the winter, there was nothing for her to do in the sun but burn. She was sick all the time, and this cost her her energy; she grew listless; she developed a matronly spread, and the vague, unfocused look of someone over forty who might be sixty—or would be, tomorrow.

All this happened to Mrs. Merrill while her children were still small; they were sickly, too. Although they were successful scholars, they were so often ill and missed so many school days that they had to repeat whole grades. Two of them were older than I was, but not a lot older; one of them was even demoted to my grade—I don't remember which one; I don't even remember which sex. That was another problem that the Merrill children suffered: they were utterly forgettable. If you didn't see the Merrill children for weeks at a time, when you saw them again, they appeared to have been replaced by different children.

The Rev. Lewis Merrill had the appearance of a plain man who, with education and intensity, had risen above his ordinariness; and his rise manifested itself in his gift of speech. But his family labored under a plainness so virulent that the dullness of his wife and children outshone even their proneness to illness, which was remarkable.

It was said that Mrs. Merrill had a drinking problem—or, at least, that her modest intake of alcohol was in terrible conflict with her long list of prescription drugs. One of the children once swallowed *all* the drugs in the house and had to have its stomach pumped. And following a kind of pep talk that Mr. Merrill gave to the youngest Sunday school class, one of his own children pulled the minister's hair and spit in his face. When the Merrill children were growing up, one of them vandalized a cemetery.

Here was our pastor, clearly bright, clearly grappling with all the most *thoughtful* elements of religious faith, and doubt; yet, clearly, God had cursed his family.

There was simply no comparable sympathy for the Rev. Dudley Wiggin—*Captain* Wiggin, some of his harsher critics called him. He was a hale and hearty type, he had a grin like a gash in his face; his smile was the smirk of a restless survivor. He looked like a former *downed* pilot, a veteran of crash landings, or shoot-outs in the sky—Dan Needham told me that Captain Wiggin had been a bomber pilot in the war, and Dan would know: he was a sergeant himself, in Italy and in Brazil, where he was a cryptographic technician. And even Dan was appalled at the crassness with which Dudley Wiggin directed the Christmas Pageant—and Dan was more tolerant of amateur theatrical performances than the average Gravesend citizen. Mr. Wiggin injected a kind of horror-movie element into the Christmas miracle; to the rector, every Bible story was—if properly understood—threatening.

And *his* wife, clearly, had not suffered. A former stewardess, Barbara Wiggin was a brash, backslapping redhead; Mr. Wiggin called her "Barb," which was how she introduced herself in various charity-inspired phone calls.

"Hi! It's Barb Wiggin! Is your mommy or your daddy home?"

She was very much a *barb*, if not a nail, in Owen's side, because she enjoyed picking him up by his pants—she would grab him by his belt, her fist in his belly, and lift him to her stewardess's face: a frankly handsome, healthy, efficient face. "Oh, you're a cute-y!" she'd tell Owen. "Don't you ever dare grow!"

9

When "My Dog, the Methodist" appeared in the Christian Century, the magazine was besieged with rebuttals, most of them humorous in spirit. However, two long-time readers indignantly asked that their names be removed from the magazine's list of subscribers.

"Will someone at Duke please find something useful for William Willimon to do?" wrote one enraged reader.

Humor is useful, even when its object is our own beloved family of believers, especially when the brunt of our humor is ourselves.

"MY DOG, THE METHODIST"*

William H. Willimon

At The United Methodist Church's most recent General Conference, we voted to make nine million new Methodists by 1992. Southern Baptists scoffed; how could a denomination that has managed to lose about 65,000 members every year somehow come up with many millions of Methodists in the next few years? Last year we couldn't even find over 200,000 new Methodists. So where do we expect to find the other nine million?

In four years at my previous parish—despite my earnest efforts to apply the principles of the Church Growth Movement—I found only about 150 new Methodists, and some of them weren't any better at being Methodist than they were being Baptist or Presbyterian or whatever they were before I found them. So I had about decided that our goal of nine million new members would make us the laughing stock of everybody in COCU. Then in the course of my scholarly duties, I came upon a brilliant but neglected monograph by Professor Charles M. Nielsen of Colgate-Rochester Divinity School titled "Communion For Dogs" (German title, *Abendmahl Für Hunde*, Perspectives in Religious Studies, Mercer University). Building upon the ground-breaking work of Peter Singer's *Animal Liberation* (Avon, 1977), and basing his thesis on all sorts of footnotes from biblical, patristic, medieval, and Reformation sources, Dr. Nielsen makes a convincing argument that dogs should be admitted to the Lord's Table in reformed churches:

> Reformed churches used to stress discipline, but now it is clear that we train our dogs far better than we train our children. . . . Since . . . dogs [are not] self-centered, ego-centric or selfish, they are now the only appropriate Christ symbols. They are loyal, adorable, loving and caring, and clearly should be allowed to receive communion.

It is fair to say that *Communion for Dogs* gives all dogs a new leash on life, so to speak.

Being a Methodist, my concern is not who should come to the Lord's Supper (which we don't celebrate that often, anyway) but where in the world we expect to find a million new members. But after reading Nielsen, I knew: right in my own home, sleeping even now in my garage, is a willing convert—Polly, a black terrier of uncertain parentage and quixotic disposition. All over this fair nation, there are many millions of Polly's compatriots who have been neglected, ignored and even scorned by evangelistic efforts. Yet they already possess all of the characteristics for membership in one of today's most progressive denominations: openness, spontaneity, affirmation, inclusiveness, love, righteous indignation, sexual freedom, gut reactions.   Here are our nine million new Methodists!

Why has the Christian church heretofore overlooked dogs as fit recipients of the Good News? The answer is simple: bigotry, closed-mindedness, and prejudice. No doubt many of you immediately call to mind Revelation 22:15, which lists those who are refused admission into the eternal bliss of heaven: "Outside are the dogs and sorcerers and fornicators and murderers and idolaters . . . "

But what does that prooftext prove? I've served churches where murderers may have been scarce, but fornicators were not. Besides, we have learned to jettison so much of Scripture with which we don't agree, why should we preserve the obviously anticanine sentiments of Revelation 22:15?

All scripture must be read by dog lovers with a "hermeneutics of suspicion"; the Bible gives dogs a bad rap. Even though Genesis 9:8-10 asserts that covenant is established, "with every living creature . . . and every beast of the earth, as many as came out of the ark," traditional exegesis has acted as if every beast and creature were on the ark except for Polly's ancestors. If Polly's ancestors hated water as much as she does when I try to give her a bath, I can assure you that no ark would have left port without dogs on board.

You will no doubt say that this anticanine prejudice merely reflects the culture-bound nature of Scripture, that we have at last overcome the bias. Don't be so sure! When Billy Graham preached at our Chapel last year, I asked him how many dogs he had converted. This man—who has gone to the ends of the earth to preach—looked at me as if I were crazy. I guess that I shouldn't have expected better of someone who admires the likes of Charles G. Finney, who wrote in his *Lectures on Revivals of Religion*:

> People should leave their dogs and very young children at home. I have often known contentions arise among dogs . . . just at that stage of the services, that would most effectually destroy the effect of the meeting. . . . As for dogs, they had infinitely better be dead, than to divert attention from the word of God. See that deacon; perhaps his dog has in this way destroyed more souls than the deacon will ever be instrumental in saving.

Even the so-called *Inclusive Language Lectionary*, while making such a fuss over the sexism and patriarchal nature of

Scripture and going to such extreme efforts to delete it from the hearing of modern, more enlightened Christian congregations—totally ignores the Bible's anticanine bias. The *Inclusive Language Lectionary* prides itself on its reworking of such passages as Hebrews 11 to read "By faith Abraham [and Sarah] obeyed when they were called to go out to a place. . . . And they went out, not knowing where they were to go." But where is the mention of Abraham and Sarah's dogs? Did the dogs who faithfully followed them into an unknown land know the route any better than Abraham and Sarah? Did their following require any less faith? No! In fact, the dogs had to have *more* faith than Abraham and Sarah since they were following human beings who admittedly had no idea of where they were going.

Of course, there will always be those who object to such hermeneutics because the original text doesn't say that Abraham (or Sarah) had a dog. But their very objection proves my point. In telling the story, backward, conservative, bourgeoisie people have completely and intentionally overlooked the contributions of dogs. Do you find dogs mentioned in the stories of Jacob, Joseph, Moses, David, Bathsheba, Esther or Ruth? I rest my case.

For the intractably reactionary, other texts must also be considered. For instance, is not my thesis that Polly is a potential Methodist vitiated by Matthew 7:6: "Do not give dogs what is holy; and do not throw pearls before swine"? Careful exegesis shows that this text cannot be taken seriously. *Kusin* is a metaphor for wicked people. Dogs here are simply not dogs.

Then there is that unfortunate slip by Paul in Philippians 3:2: "Look out for the dogs." Professor Nielsen notes that the "dogs" here were possibly Jewish Christians. Therefore, rather than being a term of opprobrium, "Look out for dogs" is an early reference to fellow Christians. "You old dog, you," when spoken by one Christian to another, is a term of endearment.

Besides, even if these texts do say nasty things about

canines, we have been so successful at removing Jesus' strictures against divorce, riches, violence, and adultery, why can't we dispose of Matthew 7:6 and Philippians 3:2 as well?

Fortunately, the exclusivistic and humanistic bias of these texts must be balanced with that beloved remark by our Lord in Mark 7:28. Nielsen is quite right in basing his central argument on Jesus' command that dogs under the table should have the children's crumbs.

Speaking of sacraments, there is clear biblical warrant for dogs as fit subjects for baptism—even though Polly hates baths. In defending infant baptism, scholars such as Oscar Cullmann and Joachim Jeremias give weight to what is called the "*oikos* formula" (from the Greek word for "household"), noting that, at a number of places in Acts, someone is baptized "and his whole household with him." Even though children are not explicitly mentioned, these great scholars assume that children were also members of the household and were therefore baptized at an early age.

Well, how many dog owners do you know who would not consider their pet to be a part of the household? We always take ours with us when we go to the beach, to the park, to the grandparents' house. Isn't it reasonable, then, to assume that the primitive church would have taken them along for baptism? We talk to dogs, kiss them, cuddle them, and toilet train them (more rapidly than we can train our children). So if children can be baptized, so can dogs. What is more, now we have progressed to the point where our dogs eat and dress like us, have beauty parlors, cemeteries, psychologists, and birth control devices—and we have become like them in our sexual behavior. So I see no biblical objection to any congregation receiving them as full communicants.

Historically, dogs like Polly have received great support from some of our best theologians. Luther, in his *Table Talk* (No. 5418) praises two dogs that performed a perfectly natural (but socially unacceptable) breakthrough, one over the grave of the Bishop of Halle and the other into a Catholic holy water pot. Dogs have been Lutherans (or Lutherans have been dogs) before we Methodists ever considered the idea.

It was also Luther who said of his little dog Toelpel, "Ah, if I could only pray the way this dog looks at meat" (*Table Talk*, No. 274). How often do you hear Luther admit that another human is a better Christian than he?

I'll admit that, at present, Polly is not exactly the moral exemplar for our neighborhood. She bitterly detests all members of the feline community, tried recently to do damage to the leg of the urologist next door when he went out unannounced to retrieve his morning paper, and seems utterly unconvinced of the value of monogamy.

But already, on any evening when the moon is full, she fulfills the invitation of Jonah 3:8: "Let man and beast . . . cry mightily to God." She cried so mightily one Tuesday evening last week that my neighbor, the urologist, threatened to do what he has heretofore declined to do: talk to an attorney. Thus Polly effected reconciliation between two adversaries, doctors and lawyers. And who should praise the Lord? Read Psalm 148:10.

In short, Polly already has all of the characteristics that would make her a wonderful Methodist.

Studies within the Church Growth Movement indicate that theology isn't an important factor in evangelism. Far more significant are warmth, enthusiasm, and feeling—all of which are so beautifully expressed by Polly and her kin.

Was it not the great theologian Friedrich Schleiermacher who defined religion as a "feeling of absolute dependence" rather than "an instinct craving for a mess of metaphysical and ethical crumbs"? Methodists are not too big on theological speculation. Similarly, I have never seen Polly bothered by metaphysical or ethical speculation. (She may indulge in such in the privacy of our garage, but I doubt it.) She knows that she is absolutely dependent on me to keep my neighbor from killing her for chasing his cat.

G. W. F. Hegel countered Schleiermacher by saying that, if religion were merely a feeling of absolute dependence, "then the dog would be the best Christian." I rest my case.

If we United Methodists give Polly the Right Hand of Fellowship and a pledge card, we'll be well on our way toward that goal of nine million new members. On second thought, forget the right hand of fellowship and just tell her how glad we are to have her in the church. Polly may have the heart of a Methodist, but she still has the teeth of a pagan.

10

The vast, ultra-modern megachurch with its egotistical, star preacher and its blend of show-biz glitz with get-em-in-at-any-cost evangelism is the object of this satire by Tom Raabe. Welcome to the world of the Rev. Dr. Roy "Solomon in a leisure suit" Dude.

"THE ULTIMATE CHURCH"*

Tom Raabe

Remember the superchurch movement of the '80s, when megachurches were in genesis and the glorification of largeness ran rampant throughout the Christian world? Remember how church-growth pastors the world over set seemingly preposterous membership goals?

How remote it all seems in the year 2005, now that last century's novas of growth have been eclipsed by a Southern California supernova, an empire builder who 23 years ago brought into existence a huge amorphous web of ecclesial polity, the logical consummation of superchurch thinking. He dubbed it the "ultra-church": First Ultra-Church of Southern California, to be precise. I am speaking, of course, of the Rev. Dr. Roy "Solomon in a leisure suit" Dude.

Forget Korea, Taiwan and Brazil; disregard Lynchburg, Hammond and Garden Grove. First Ultra of Southern California makes the Crystal Cathedral look like a house church. It lays claim to 2.5 million souls. It adds about 10,000 new members to its roles every month, 333 per day, 13.9 per hour and one every five minutes. Dude has 166,279 cell groups, 172,346 deacons and 12,820 full-time staff (9,543 of which are ordained clergy). The numbers are beyond comprehension: average Sunday worship attendance is 552,364, a figure amassed in 11 services averaging over 50,000 each. Worship is enhanced by 431 choirs, 25 orchestral groups, 30 children's choirs and 16 handbell choirs. Festival day processions look like the Rose Parade.

Dude's yearly "backdoor loss" is the size of a small denomination. I—along with 29 of my fellows—sat reeling in this vertiginous onslaught of numbers, thrown at us courtesy of a videocassette detailing the history and goals of First Ultra. In fact, each of us had one in hand as part of the opulent "visitor recognition package" presented to each first-time visitor. (The climax of the proceedings comes at the end of each Sunday service when one tag is drawn from a hopper of visitor name tags and a new car is given to that visitor.)

We sat in the Love Room, clad in black slickers with three-inch high white letters spelling "LOVE" on the back and awaiting our guide for the 9:00 A.M. Love Tour.

Along with the grounds and facilities, it was the tour guide I wanted to see. Being an ex-usher myself, I took considerable interest in Head Usher Simon Glibface, the brains behind the revolutionary visitor recognition program at First Ultra. The man had grown to legendary stature in conservative Christianity. Indeed, when is the last time you've seen an usher featured on the cover of *Christianity Today*? ("The Sensation with the Carnation: The Ultimate Usher for the Ultimate Church," March 16, 1998.) With his subsequent usher textbooks, autobiography (*There Is Life Beyond Name Tags*, Dude Books, 2001), magazine (*Badge and Bulletin*, the only ushering magazine including a centerfold portrait) and cultlike following, Glibface had almost singlehandedly brought ushering into the sunlight of ecclesiastical celebrity. To his fame are credited such innovative strategies as parking valets, tour guides, computerized seating readouts for latecomers, and Roy Dude University's School of Usherology. The man had revolutionized the field. It was his brainstorm to coordinate the corps by color-coded tuxedos: sky blue for the parking valets, lime green for the greeters and bumblebee yellow for the transportation corps. To keep his finger on the pulse at First Ultra, Glibface traditionally gave the 9:00 A.M. Love Tour.

When he stepped through the door with the conclusion of the video at promptly 8:58 A.M., a shiver swept the room. It is one of the sensations one recognizes immediately at megachurches, one of the permutations of the secular manifested onto the religious—a nimbus of celebrity that hangs above those in power. Were Dude himself to stride through the door, the hushing would be augmented exponentially. Dude has taken the role of superchurch preacher to its logical end. Nobody expects a man like Dude to be pastoral. Nobody expects him to counsel or remember names or recall faces. If Dude spent ten minutes with each of his parishioners, the task would consume his every min- ute—waking and sleeping—for more than 49 years. No, when church growth overwhelmed the evangelical market back in the '80s, the superchurch became the goal, the prize to be won. Seminary students no longer wanted to shepherd—they wanted to ranch. And men like Dude transcended even the status of rancher; they became kings.

Glibface asked if we wouldn't mind walking. Although eight other tours staggered two minutes apart from 9:02 to 9:16 A.M. would ride in electric 30-seat carts and listen to guides through personal headsets, it had been a Glibface tradition since the inception of the Love Tour to take his group on foot. In a throwback to a simpler day, he spoke with no amplification.

The man was smooth. When I first learned of the color-coding system at First Ultra, I thought it the tawdriest thing to hit the church at large since colored clerical collars. But then I had not seen Glibface. The $90 razor haircut, the surgically improved visage, the tan—the man oozed Califor- nia; he was golden-tongued, and yet not totally yielding to smarm. He played, still, off the perception that this was a church, not the Vegas strip. Let the church take from the commercial world all it will—marketing techniques, parking philosophy—but let it call itself a church. And the color-coding taken as part of the package fit. It worked.

We strolled onto the gangway, high above the 52,000-seat sanctuary. Through glass windows we could view, seven stories below, the foyer on our right, and on the left, the sanctuary, filling rapidly to capacity. Upbeat, rhythmic music filled the sanctuary as two 4,000-member choirs, one clad in fire-engine red robes, the other in silver, swayed in chorus to words flashed on two of five 60-foot Jumbo-o-Tron screens. The song leader—a mere ant with waving arms from where we stood—loomed larger than life on three other screens. Everybody sang. High-speed ramps whisked latecomers to their seats. Dude would "appear" later, Glibface said. Dude preached 46 Sundays a year, or at least a three dimensional 40-foot-by-20-foot laser image of Dude's head did. Dude himself never showed.

First Ultra had subscribed to the multicongregational superchurch model, Glibface explained, offering distinctive worship experiences catering to differing tastes. Thus, six services were in the Reformed tradition—three informal, three traditional—four services were charismatic, and, as a sop to the creedal, confessional, liturgical, sacramental types—I was one of those—they offered the "9:00 P.M. hour."

"Communion must take days," I marveled, envisioning 52,000 marching down for the common cup. "Not quite," Glibface returned. "We found that communion cut into our attendance by as much as 40,000, and the services still ran well into the wee hours. Once we sang an entire hymnal, one verse of each, during the distribution. Of course, that was before Dr. Dude decided on the auxiliary stations." Glibface swept his arm over the perimeter of the sanctuary. "Forty-foot doors open and complete chancels slide forward with ministers and everything all set up. There are 18 of those. Of course the speed ramps help. Nobody walks. A person can get from the back row to the altar in 23.7 seconds.

But, now . . . " he bade us move on as 30 people clad in black "JOY" slickers entered the gangway.

"What about baptisms?" a woman asked as our faces were pulled back from the G-force exerted against them on the high-speed escalator that whooshed us to main level. "We do those in late spring," Glibface said. "We used to simply haul everybody over to Playa del Ray or El Segundo and do it in the ocean, but the city fathers squawked about extra lifeguards and whatnot, plus 10,000 to 20,000 people in white robes invading the beach area freaked out the surfers, so we decided to keep to our 100-meter, fully landscaped reflecting pool behind the altar." He looked specifically at me. "For the sacramental hour, 12 fonts pop up hydraulically on the sides of the chancel."

He led us into the "Cry Room." Rows and rows of cribs stretched toward the horizon. "Three thousand crib capacity, with one-way windows and acoustically perfect sound," Glibface was saying as we watched thousands of mothers seated beside their babies listening to the service through headsets. "We have on hand 16,000 rattles, 4,000 dolls, 2,000 washettes, and 4,000 crib mobiles. That facility there," he pointed toward a monstrous bin, "has the capacity to process 50,000 diapers a day."

Now the largest church in the world, a religious organization to dwarf even that of the mighty Cho—guru to millions in the Korean revival of the '80s and '90s—First Ultra-Church of Southern California is the quintessential church-growth success story.

Dispatched from seminary fresh-faced and spitting into his hands, a fighting-the-forces-of-smallness dynamo, Roy Dude arrived in 1982 with the charge of starting a mission in the beach community adjacent to Los Angeles International Airport. In a move that made his peers look like disciples of negativism, Dude immediately named his yet-to-be established congregation the First Ultra-Church of Southern California. He billed himself as the greatest possibility thinker since Elijah; the greatest builder since Solomon. He conducted weekly television services from a rented recording studio. (Schuller at least had preached to people in cars.) Dude preached to no one, yet his technological mastery was so facile that, via adept video splicing and sound effects, his broadcast presented an eerie verisimilitude of the real thing, an eeriness that carries over to this day.

Only after he had received the first 1,000 phone calls, then and only then, did he conduct an actual, live worship service before actual, live worshipers. No tedious pounding on doors and inviting people to church; no struggling through tough days in elementary school media centers; no hand-to-mouth existence. None of that for Roy Dude. He started big and kept getting bigger.

By 1991 Dude had constructed a 10,000-seat sanctuary and set his sights on outdrawing the Los Angeles Dodgers—a goal realized the next year, a year the Dodgers went to the Series. In 1995 he purchased the Los Angeles International Airport when LAX moved to its current home on landfill five miles off the coast (downwind from the 2,000-foot smog fans). One year later, faith projections were seeing reality in the present 52,000-seat sanctuary known colloquially as "the Dudedome."

Glibface had opportunity to gloss the high points in the First Ultra story as we exited the cry room and gathered about him in the middle of an enormous cavern that, once worship was over, would be instantly transformed into the coffee and fellowship area with—I had to ask—8,000 coffee urns. We turned a corner in the enormous foyer and saw a huge sign that read, "To the trains," with an arrow pointing to the right; another reading "To the sanctuary" pointed left. Interior directional signs. Amazing! Basic church-growth principles employed even at this level.

Once aboard, Glibface told the story of the trains, a tale he termed "one of the greatest triumphs over the forces of negativism in the history of the Christian church," and it dealt with the single most inviolable principle in all of church growth: All is negotiable save one thing—parking. Once the lots are 80 percent full, it's time for expansion.

"For five years we ringed the sanctuary with lots," Glibface said. "And when those were filled, we paved lots behind them, and more behind them. Finally, in 2001, attendance plateaued at 1.8 million. And curiously, our lots were only at 71 percent capacity. It was a crisis time for First Ultra. Dr. Dude prayed and fasted for a week on Mt. Baldy and when he came down he imparted to us the Principle of Distance Strangulation: People will not willingly walk more than .75 miles from parking spot to sanctuary. At a ballgame, maybe. At church, no way. We had near-empty lots sitting a mile from church. Obviously, some type of surface mass transportation system was needed. Dr. Dude toyed with purchasing surplus Army helicopters—they seat 55. But finally he chose light rail. We experienced a little backdoor loss from that—200,000 members. But we gained that number back in no time."

The train had come to rest in front of a building. I could see the sign "Faith Tower." I craned my neck for a look up. Faith Tower, one of four 40-story monoliths—the others were Hope, Charity and Hezekiah Towers—stood at the eastern terminus of the rail system; it was testimony to Dude's emphasis on education and cell groups. He had 13,794 Sunday school classes spread throughout the four towers in classes ranging from five students to 6,000, with an average ratio of one teacher to 20 students.

We stepped through the sparkling unloading station—Christian Muzak urging us on—and into the lobby of Faith Tower, where phalanxes of red-clad adjutants lined the walls awaiting the opportunity to assist. Coffee urns ringed the foyer. Bibles were stacked—seemingly in unlimited supply—for those who failed to bring their own. A huge, four-sided electronic sign stood in the middle listing the myriad classes scheduled, their location, whether seating was available and where the vacant seats were located according to a digitized floor plan. We peeked into Room 1A, a 6,000-seat auditorium on the first floor, before filing out of the tower's south entrance onto a lush grassy area the size of a football field, strewn with benches and tables, the ubiquitous fountains, waterfalls, ornamental lakes, statuary and reflecting pools. Rising prominently at the east end of this plain was some exemplary topiary—bushes fashioned into 30-foot figures of the apostles (a sort of shrubbery version of St. Peter's in Rome). . . . A breezy stroll through the printing plant revealed two huge presses in full operation, printing next Sunday's bulletin. Then Glibface took us into what appeared at first sight to be the NASA Space Control Center. A huge darkened room spread below us, with banks and banks of television monitors, an attendant at each, all concentrically arranged around a gigantic illuminated map of Los Angeles. We walked along a gangway as Glibface talked. This was the "War Room." Demographic data had been plotted on the central map with saturation areas denoted by one color and blinking lights all around the L.A. area by others—each light representing 10,000 members. On the computer screens, workers were pulling up neighborhood profiles, cell group configurations, Bible class listings.

"Taking attendance must be a chore," I said, again thinking of logistics. Glibface plunged into the details. Two mainframes and 1,500 people working round-the-clock from early Monday through mid-Wednesday every week were necessary to take attendance—church, Bible class and cell group. Anyone missing three consecutive times receives a note in the mail. Miss a fourth and a deacon is at the door. It made perfect sense. When numbers are your *raison d'etre,* you must pay the price to get those numbers. Knowing that you reach millions is hardly enough. Cold numbers are the key.

But we were running late. The 9:00 A.M. service would be dismissed in mere minutes. *That* was something I, in my logistical caprice, longed to see. Fifty-two thousand parishioners coming out of church and 52,000 different ones going in. I expected to witness something akin to the last five minutes of Pompeii. Lucky this was not the Midwest in winter, with 52,000 pairs of boots and rubbers thrown into the mix.

While speeding through a tunnel of luxuriant palms on our way back to Sanctuary Station, I decided to pop the million-dollar question: "What of community?" I asked. "Does anybody know anybody else?" Surely, this was the apotheosis of numbers for numbers' sake—the fulfillment of prophetic voices from the mainline of the 1980s.

Glibface had heard the plaint many times over. His eyes sparked as he leveled me in his sights and proceeded to offer the well-worn 60-member argument. In any congregation of any size the maximum number in a friendship circle is 60, he said. There are 60 you know by name, 60 you visit, 60 who constitute your group. All others are strangers, or close to it. "In the multicongregational structure," he explained, "the Bible class serves as the fellowship format. The people you know and love gather there."

"But then First Ultra is not one church, but many little churches," I said. "To claim the grandiose numbers is playing the ultimate numbers game."

"Oh, we do have congregational events," Glibface returned. "Last year's church picnic was spectacular. We caravaned out to the high desert. One hundred thousand cars on Interstate 15. The entire fleet of Sunday school buses (1,582 54-seat school buses). We had Christian singers, Christian entertainment acts. The biggest church picnic ever. Four hundred seventy tons of potato salad on hand. Two hundred thousand gallons of grapesoda, 67,000 father-son softball games, 55,000 co-ed volleyball games, 3 million water balloons . . . "

I waved my arms in surrender, hoping to stanch this logorrheic flow, this tour de force of numerolatry. But, alas, to no avail.

" . . . and, for the first time in First Ultra history, we broke the 2 million mark in bratwursts. And, of course, the event had its spiritual side too. Our annual exercise in proclamation evangelism was an unrivaled success. Every person had a placard with one word of the Bible on it, five feet by two feet. We proclaimed Scripture word for word all the way to Hosea

13. Almost stretched to Needles. Next year we're shooting for the entire Old Testament."

Glibface inhaled, a prolepsis of more numerological effluvium, but we had arrived at Sanctuary Station. The tour had ended. Streams of people sped past the windows of our halted car, in transit either to the sanctuary, the Sunday School complex, or the adjacent esplanade, a porticoed promenade lined with shops and stalls offering the latest in ecclesiastical amenities. One store sold Roy Dude teaching tapes, another Roy Dude preaching tapes, another Roy Dude books, another Dudedome snow globes. There was a library, a bookstore, a credit union, a barber shop, and, to accommodate the yen of the hungry First Ultra parishioner, 52 restaurants.

Glibface offered us a genial send-off. We handed our slickers to a janissary at the door (who subsequently rushed them to the Love Room for the 10:30 A.M. Love Tour), stepped off the train, negotiated the phalanx of greeters that had mustered for us—we were each met by a personal escort at the end of the phalanx—and were thus shunted off in whatever direction we wanted.

I wanted breakfast. I hurried toward the esplanade and Roy Dude Restaurant Row. I would miss the service, yes, but—well, there's a Sunday every week. Besides, where else can you get immediate seating at 10:00 A.M. on a Sunday?

11

Church growth can occur in many forms. If we can't baptize dogs or attain the mega-church status of the Rev. Roy Dude, what about a leveraged buyout of the Methodists by the Moravians? The following article concerns what happens when church business becomes monkey business.

Moravian pastor E. Hampton Morgan, Jr. wrote this piece for his church newsletter during the controversial leveraged buyout of RJR Nabisco. "A number of the members of my church were then employed by RJR, and I thought some take-off humor might help lighten their spirits." The article then made the rounds in national Moravian publications.

Morgan was dismayed to hear from a fellow Moravian pastor that, during his church's annual financial campaign, a member had read the article, taken it seriously, and said to his pastor, "If the Moravian Church has that much money, you don't need my pledge!"

"MORAVIANS OFFER $7.55 BILLION FOR METHODISTS"*

E. Hampton Morgan, Jr.

In a move that sent shock waves through ecclesiastical circles nationwide, the Moravian Church, Southern Province, announced a $7.55 billion offer for The United Methodist Church, the nation's second largest Protestant denomination.

Officials of the Southern Province, which has a total membership of 22,000 and is based in Winston-Salem, North Carolina, said the offer of $7.55 billion amounted to a bid of

$200,000 for each of the 37,750 United Methodist congrega-
tions in the United States and Puerto Rico.

Sources close to the Moravian Church described the
takeover attempt as a leveraged buyout. This highly
successful technique of the business world usually involves
the sale of some of the assets of the target company to repay
the loans made to finance the purchase. This is the first
instance such a technique has been used by a church.

Moravian insiders speculated that the Southern Baptist
Convention, with ambitious growth goals of its own, might be
eager to purchase anywhere from 25 percent to 50 percent of
the Methodist congregations. This would enable the
Moravian Church to come out of the deal debt-free and with a
membership increase of at least 25,000 percent. The status of
the Southern Baptist Convention would also be enhanced,
but on a smaller scale.

A Moravian bishop, however, said he favored operating
The United Methodist Church as a wholly-owned subsidiary
of the Moravian Church for at least five years before selling
any of its congregations. "Let us just call it Zinzendorf's
revenge," he said. The bishop declined to explain the
meaning of his statement.

Church growth analysts at Fuller Theological Seminary saw
the move as a bold attempt by one of the nation's smallest
denominations to fulfill long-held dreams of numerical growth
and a presence in all 50 states. A professor of Church Growth at
Fuller was quoted as saying the Moravian move was one of the
most innovative church growth initiatives he had ever seen. "It
would appear," he said, "that the Moravians are seeking to
rewrite the book on church growth."

Experts on Wall Street suggested that the Moravian
takeover attempt was probably an angry reaction by
Winston-Salem residents to the buyout of Piedmont Airlines
in 1987 by U.S. Air and the recent multibillion dollar offers
for RJR Nabisco. Piedmont Airlines and RJR Nabisco are both
based in Winston-Salem. "Who would've ever guessed," said
one Wall Street analyst, "that Winston-Salem natives would

fight back this way?" Wall Street brokers also suggested that the Moravian takeover move was a smart financial decision. "Total denominational giving to The United Methodist Church is $350 million a year," said one analyst. "With that kind of cash flow now going to the Moravian provincial office," he said, "their financial problems are surely over."

Officials of the National Council of Churches of Christ in New York expressed cautious approval of the Moravian buyout offer. One spokesperson said that prayers for Christian unity are obviously being answered, but in a completely unexpected way.

A grim, tightlipped spokesperson for The United Methodist Church's national office in Nashville declined to answer reporters' questions.

12

The peril of being God is the theme for humor essayist Calvin Trillin. In this piece Trillin worries about the prayer life of some of the members of the Reagan Administration and the possibility of "Diety Overload." This essay originally appeared in "Uncivil Liberties," Trillin's popular column for The Nation.

"TOO SOON TO TELL"*

Calvin Trillin

I had assumed that during this month—the traditional time for midterm toting up, national stocktaking, and Washington thumb-sucking—people would be asking me a lot of questions about Deity Overload. These kinds of questions: Has the period of the most acute danger of Deity Overload passed? Has the economy become a factor? How do you see Deity Overload affecting the Western alliance? Will Deity Overload be a major factor in the second half of Ronald Reagan's term? Will Ronald Reagan be a major factor in the second half of Ronald Reagan's term?

I was ready for them. "To pose the question in terms of 'liberal' or 'conservative' is to misunderstand it" was one of the answers I had worked up. "It's too soon to tell" was another. "It's too soon to tell" is one of my favorite answers for any question; it's that rare phrase that permits you to sound more informed by saying you don't know. Just the other day, one of my daughters said, "How do you find the area of an isosceles triangle, Daddy?" and I said, "It's too soon to tell." If cornered on the Deity Overload issue, I was prepared to go all

---

*"To Soon to Tell" by Calvin Trillin, excerpted from *With All Disrespect*, published by Ticknor & Fields. Copyright © 1985 by Calvin Trillin.

the way: I was prepared to say, "One simply doesn't know."

Nobody has asked me about Deity Overload. Maybe they think Deity Overload will obviously have no effect on the Western alliance or that the period of the most acute danger passed months ago. Or maybe they're asking someone else. Maybe they forgot that I was the one who first called attention to the danger of Deity Overload. The public memory is short, after all. Just the other night, as I was eating a plate of picadillo with black beans and rice on the side, it occurred to me that everyone has forgotten about the Russian combat brigade in Cuba, only sixty miles off our shore. Nobody has even mentioned those Russians in years. For all we know, they might have reached Miami by now. As it happens, Miami these days is the sort of place where a Russian combat brigade could show up without attracting much attention. If they're still in Cuba, aren't they getting homesick? Do they try to get a little taste of Mother Russia by having half of the brigade stand in long lines for the wrong size shoes while the other half throws snow on them? Where do they get the snow? It's too soon to tell.

It might be advisable to remind everyone precisely how the danger of Deity Overload first came to public attention. I did it, all my myself. This was at the beginning of the Reagan Administration, when there were a lot of stories going around about how James Watt, a committed Christian who had been appointed Secretary of Drilling, considered no matter too small to benefit from a prayerful request for divine guidance. This, if you'll try to remember, was just after the Reverend Jerry Falwell had asked God to help the Moral Majority defeat a bunch of Congressmen who were blasphemers, drunkards, idolaters, and, on their better days, fornicators. It occurred to me that God already had, as the British ambassador might put it, a lot on His plate.

Was I denying the omnipotence of the Divine Being? To state the question in those terms is to misunderstand it. I was not saying that God has any limits on His powers, only on His patience. I fully understood that Watt might need divine guidance on the big issues. If there came a time, for instance, when he had to decide whether to turn Zion National Park over to Exxon or to preserve it for Mobil, it seemed reasonable for him to ask for a little help. What worried me was the thought that Watt might be asking for divine intervention when he wasn't sure how much of a raise to give his driver or was trying to decide whether wearing a cowboy hat on a trip to Montana might persuade people that he was not, in fact, a wonk.

Here is God, as I envision it, dealing with the usual—five or six wars, a flood here, pestilence there, a billion or two serious commandment-breakers. He's got Jehovah's Witnesses and Seventh-Day Adventists jabbering away at Him day and night. Falwell is pressing for a day-of-rest easement to give Congressmen PAC money on the Sabbath. In the midst of all this, here comes James Watt to ask about cowboy hats. Would it be surprising if, at that point, God said, "Enough's enough"? That would be Deity Overload.

So has the most acute danger of Deity Overload passed, now that the parks are safely in the hands of the oil companies and Jerry Falwell seems to have joined the Russian combat brigade in Cuba? No. The economy has become a factor. A lot of people now have the need for divine intervention in matters that rank in importance somewhere between war and cowboy hats. Given the state of the economy, I can imagine plenty of people saying something like, "If you can't save my store, God, could you at least give the discounter across the street psoriasis?"

And the implications of the international situation? Good question. The implications are enormous. Every morning Ayatollah Khomeini comes in to present God with the news that fifteen or twenty people were executed the previous night for His greater glory—giving God the names of a banker here and a university professor there, the way an overeager cocker spaniel might drop dead sparrows at the feet of its master. Then Menachem Begin appears to remind God about His promise of all Judea and Samaria. "Yes, I know there were a lot of gods in those days," Begin says, "but you were definitely the one we talked to." He is waved away, but reappears almost immediately, saying, "Remember—*all* Judea and Samaria. All of Judea. Also all of Samaria. Did I mention milk and honey?" There are fourteen wars going on. From Cuba, several hundred Russian soldiers and Jerry Falwell are trying to make a deal with God to trade their immortal souls for not having to listen to one more four-hour speech by Fidel Castro. Khomeini shows up again with the corpses of our four newspaper editors and a labor leader. Begin is holding a map that shows Samaria to have extended to the suburbs of Istanbul. Watt is asking whether the cowboy hat may not simply make him look like rough trade. Has the point of Deity Overload been reached? One simply doesn't know.

13

In the course of Art Buchwald's never-ending attempts to puncture the egos of the politically pompous, he occasionally wanders into the area of religion. When he does, Buchwald's efforts are typically hilarious. The following selections of Buchwald's religious wit show him having a fun time with three undeniably serious subjects—the Pope in Poland, modern marriage, and prayer in schools.

SELECTIONS FROM
YOU CAN FOOL ALL OF THE PEOPLE ALL OF THE TIME

Art Buchwald

"HOLY FATHER"

The Polish Central Committee had an emergency meeting as soon as the Pope's plane took off from Krakow to return to Rome.

"All right," one of the high officials said. "Who came up with the smart idea to have the Pope visit Poland?"

Someone pointed his finger at Panowski.

Panowski threw up his hands. "I thought it would be good for tourism. You have to admit we got great press all over the world."

"Especially in Moscow," one of the members said. "Do you realize what you've done, Panowski? You brought all the Solidarity people back together again, you allowed them to have demonstrations in the street, and we may have to lift martial law."

"How did I know there were that many Catholics in the country?"

"You could have asked us, Panowski. Would you mind telling us exactly how you got us into this mess?"

"Well, last winter I got a call from the Vatican, and the man said that the Pope would like to visit his homeland. I thought he wanted to go to the village where he was born and have a few days' rest at a monastery. I didn't know he was going to use the trip to bring a message to the Polish people."

"You think the Pope just goes around the world looking for a place to take a vacation?"

"I expected him to say Mass, but I didn't realize anybody would show up for it."

"Only ten million people showed up, Panowski."

"But they didn't all take communion."

"I think you're missing the point, Panowski. Until the Pope's visit we had the unions under control, the people were dispirited and had lost their will to fight us, and we looked as if we were in control. Now everything is changed and we're back where we started. The Pope gave everyone a shot in the arm, which is something we didn't need at this time."

"So I underestimated his appeal as a spiritual leader. We all make mistakes."

"Is that what you want us to tell Moscow?"

"Why do we have to tell Moscow anything? We're an independent country."

"No reason except they have six million troops on our border. You better come up with a good story when the Kremlin calls us, which should be any minute now."

"Why don't we say he came here on a trade mission to buy Polish hams, in exchange for Vatican wheat?"

"I'm not sure the Soviets will buy that one; after the speeches he made from the pulpit."

"We could say that the Western press exaggerated the visit

and made it into a political spectacle to further their warlike intentions toward the Warsaw Pact nations."

"That's better, but it's still not good enough. The Soviets are going to ask why we let him come in the first place."

"Because we needed the hard currency to buy oil from the Russians?"

"It won't fly, Panowski."

The phone started ringing.

"It's them, Panowski. Why don't you answer it?"

"Hello, yes, Comrade. This is the Central Committee. Before you say anything, he's gone. We kicked him out of the country before he could do any damage. . . . No, no. Everything's quiet in Poland. Do you think that one priest could be a threat to the great Polish Communist Party? . . . Who told you the whole country turned out to hear him? . . . That's disinformation put out by the CIA. The man didn't even fill up one small church. A few old ladies came out to see him. You have my word for it. . . . Listen to me. . . . We don't need any troops. . . . He didn't influence any of us . . . so help me God!"

"TILL DIVORCE DO US PART"

The prenuptial contract is getting more and more prevalent as the divorce rate rises in the country. Since getting married in many cases is not one of those things you do forever, lawyers are advising their clients to make out a contract specifying who gets what when love flies out the window and recrimination knocks down the door.

I was the best man at a prenuptial legal-contract ceremony the other day. The groom to be, Horace Pipeline, was attended by the famed divorce lawyer Roy Bone, and the bride to be, the lovely Grace Willowy, was being given away by Stephanie Tuff of the firm Rock, Sock & Needham.

The bride and groom sat in the love seat in Mr. Bone's palatial office, which, for the occasion, had been decorated with magnolias and white roses.

Mr. Bone, reading from a yellow legal pad, said, "Dearly

beloved, we are gathered here today to bring this man and this woman together in a happy prenuptial contract, spelling out the property claims of both parties in case, for reasons we shall not go into here, this marriage is broken asunder. Do you, Horace Pipeline, agree that, in case you do not choose to continue in wedlock, you will bestow on your lovely bride a lump sum equal to five percent of your present assets, excluding your boat, your penthouse, and your home in Southampton?"

"Wait a minute," said Miss Tuff. "Who said anything about a lump sum, and who said anything about excluding Mr. Pipeline's boat, penthouse, and home in Southampton? My client, under law, is entitled to fifty percent of all of her husband's property. But we don't want to be greedy about this. We'll settle for ten thousand dollars a month until she gets married again."

"Alimony is out of the question," Mr. Bone said. "I cannot permit my client to enter the sacred institution of matrimony unless he can get out of it by paying off a lump sum at the dissolution of the marriage. How can we be sure when and if Miss Willowy will get married again?"

"How do you feel about it, Grace?" Miss Tuff asked.

"I love Horace very much, and if he wants to provide me with a lump sum, I don't have any objection. But I want to know what numbers we're talking about before I say, 'I do.'"

Mr. Bone smiled. "You're a reasonable young lady. Would five hundred thousand satisfy you?"

Miss Tuff said, "No, it wouldn't, Roy, and you know that before we came here we researched Horace's assets down to the last nickel. Now let's be serious or call off this prenuptial legal-contract ceremony right now."

Mr. Bone scowled. "As Horace's lawyer I can't go over five hundred thousand, but if he wants to be more generous I'll leave it to him. Horace, what do you think?"

"Grace is the only woman I've ever loved," Horace said. "I can't imagine anything but death parting us. But just in case something did happen, I'm willing to give her a cool million—the same as I gave my second wife."

Miss Tuff said, "Horace's second wife was much older than Grace, and the million he settled on her was before inflation set in. We want one million five and the house in Southampton."

"It's just not possible," Mr. Bone said angrily. "These people hope to live happily ever after. My client would not have a day of happiness if he knew it would cost him a million five plus the house in Southampton to get out of the marriage."

Miss Tuff said, "How do you think my client would feel if she knew she could be tossed out in the street for a lousy million dollars?"

Grace became upset. "This talk is so sordid, it's destroying our love for each other. I'll take a million two hundred thousand and the penthouse in New York. But that's the bottom line."

Horace said, "Don't be angry, darling. You're asking for more than I planned to give you, but I want you to be happy. Give it to her, Roy, provided we have it in writing so she doesn't go to court and try to sock it to me for anything more."

"All right, Horace, it's your money. I'll have this typed up while we open a bottle of champagne and drink a toast to the happy couple. Please excuse my tears. Prenuptial marriage-contract ceremonies always make me cry."

"GOD AND SCHOOL PRAYERS"

I don't talk to God as often as I should because I know how busy He is these days. But every four years, during the presidential campaign, I do check in to make sure what the candidates are saying about Him is true.

After hearing President Reagan say for the umpteenth time that God has been expelled from America's classrooms, I asked Him, "Are You banned from America's schools?"

"Not that I know of," God replied.

"President Reagan said that kids can't pray in school."

"I don't know about that, but I hear schoolchildren's prayers all day long. Of course I hear more from those who haven't done their homework, or have been caught committing some infraction that will send them to the principal's office. And there is a lot of praying when report cards are sent home, and when college test scores come in. I can't understand why President Reagan said I've been banned from the classroom."

"I think he was referring to the Supreme Court decision which forbade organized prayer in public schools at the beginning of the day. Did that decision bother You?"

"On the contrary. I don't believe in people praying if they don't mean it. Fortunately in America people can pray any time and anywhere they want to."

"Well, why would President Reagan say that You were banned from public schools if You weren't?"

"I have no idea," God said. "People are always dropping my name in order to get votes during an election year. Frankly, I wish the President would have checked with Me first, before he misspoke."

"Do you believe it's a good idea to have separation of Church and State?"

"I believe it's an excellent one. Your country has survived for over two hundred years without getting Me mixed up in your government, and when you look around you seem to have more freedom of worship than any other place on the face of the earth. There are certain countries, which I'd rather not mention, where the leaders use My name to commit some of the most heinous crimes known to mankind."

"How would You feel about forced voluntary prayer in the schools in the morning, so if kids didn't want to pray they wouldn't have to?"

"It would bother Me. All My children are very fragile, and it would cause tremendous friction between those who prayed and those who didn't. I would prefer that school-children pray when the spirit moves them, and not when a teacher tells them to. What your President should know is

110

that God is everywhere, and when he states that I am no longer in the public schools, he doesn't know what in the devil he's talking about."

"Then You didn't tell him You wanted prayers officially back in the schools?"

"I certainly did not," God told me. "But I did talk to him about the asbestos problem."

"The asbestos problem?"

"It's very serious. A great many schools have asbestos peeling off the ceilings and walls, and it's getting into the schoolchildren's lungs, and they can die from it. I suggested that the President institute a crash program to see that the little children were protected from this terrible disease. But to My knowledge he hasn't mentioned it yet. If I were the President of the United States, I'd be much more concerned about the health of America's children than with what time of day they could pray."

"Well, thanks for Your time," I said. "I didn't want to bother You, but I was afraid that if I was against mandatory prayer in public schools You would think I didn't believe in You anymore. Could I put this conversation on the record?"

"Be my guest. There is too much talk by politicians about what I want and don't want and, as God, it really ticks Me off."

14

Since growing up as a Southern Baptist, life has become more complicated for Suzanne Britt. Although she is now more sophisticated than she was as a child in North Carolina, she has learned to appreciate her religious roots. She now helps others to write at Baptist-owned Meredith College in Raleigh, North Carolina.

"BEING BAPTIST"*

Suzanne Britt

I wrote this essay in response to the remark by the president of the Southern Baptist Convention—namely, that God does not hear the prayers of Jews. My theory is that if God can hear the prayers of Southern Baptists, God can hear the prayers of anybody.

O ne of the things it's getting more and more embarrassing to be is a Southern Baptist. I'm one. We are as common as loblolly pines. The chances of growing up Baptist in the South are as great as the probability of a Southerner's knowing the definition of, and actually *liking*, red-eye gravy.

Being a Baptist is not something I went out and picked like I'd pick a husband or a pair of designer jeans. Being a Baptist goes with the territory, sort of like preferring my iced tea already sweetened and knowing beyond a shadow of a doubt my proper station in life.

I never thought I'd feel the need to defend or justify being a Baptist, any more than I'd have to explain what constitutes

---

*Reprinted by permission of the author.

112

good blood. But lately I've been thinking maybe I'd better marshal some arguments, what with the rest of the world watching nervously as Baptists converge on Washington, invade the airwaves and run for public office. The rest of the world is listening while the head of the Southern Baptist Convention explains which prayers God hears. Many minorities and atheists are getting their feelings hurt.

I think it's time everyone understood why being a Baptist is not a club I can or should drop out of, even if the idea looks tempting. Bertrand Russell once explained why he was not a Christian. Let me tell you why I am still a Baptist.

I am still a Baptist because Baptists are fun to be. Baptists make good journalistic copy. They are always in the news because they are always making news, whether for good or ill. The pallid pronouncements of a Presbyterian are not worth repeating. But when a Baptist says something, it is really awful. It is front-page stuff.

Then, too, Baptists are so bad that when they accidentally slip up and do something good, that event also lands on the front page. You just never can tell about Baptists. They are liable, at any time and entirely without warning, to act Christian. Watching Baptists in action is more exciting than watching presidential elections and volcanic eruptions. We are a blast.

I am still a Baptist because Baptists still have beliefs. Of course, the strong possibility exists that Baptists might be wrong, but Baptists would never tell. Such arrogance is refreshing. In a world where everything is decided by committee and nobody has an opinion, Baptists are still jumping off the fence and landing in the mud every day. Baptists take risks. They give no thought to their own safety when they are keeping the world safe for morality. Baptists mean business. They are like Jews and Catholics in that respect. Flannery O'Connor, one of my favorite opinionated Catholics, said you could scratch an Episcopalian and find anything underneath. Not so with Baptists. Scratch a Baptist, and you will find the inerrant word of God, or worse.

But though Baptists are prophetic, they are also realistic. They never get confused about public and private morals. Baptists will do almost anything as long as nobody finds out about it. They will show you the same discreet courtesy. They don't really care if you run naked through the house. They just don't want you to do it until after the children are in bed.

What Baptists refuse to see won't hurt them or you. They will understand if you are a bride-taking, whisky-sipping, dancing sinner. They just think you should keep quiet about it. Baptists don't go looking for trouble. In fact, they understand better than most people the evils lurking in the human heart. But when immorality goes public, they are compelled to fly righteously into indignation. You've got to give them credit. They don't stand idly on the promises of an abstract god.

But what I love best about Baptists is how bad they are. They are boldly bad in a world where being bad is frequently glossed over. Robert Frost said Earth was the right place for love, since he didn't know where it was likely to go better. I feel the same way about being Baptist. Each time Baptists commit another outrageous sin and the world calls them on it, I ask myself where would Baptists be if not in the world. There's no escaping them.

Baptists already have everything human nature has to offer, only they have it bigger and better than anybody else. Baptists have high symbolic value. Nobody is meaner than a Baptist. Nobody is more well-intentioned than a Baptist. Nobody is more intolerant than a Baptist. Nobody is more saved than a Baptist. Nobody causes more trouble than a Baptist. Nobody is funnier than a Baptist.

I feel about being Baptist the way I feel about being human: burdened but cheerful. Nought save death can relieve me from the weight of being both.

"GUIDEPOSTS"

I have had my knuckles rapped for taking the wrong tone about my in-laws. My only response is that the tone probably wasn't wrong enough. Also, I am a writer and the only people I can think of to write about are the ones who populate my life. That includes me. You will find me taking the wrong tone about me in sentence two of this essay. I do not discriminate. I pick on everybody. Besides, I love Guideposts *better than I love beer and cheese nacho Doritos.*　　Suzanne Britt

Every year my in-laws give me another subscription to *Guideposts* magazine. They are still, after fifteen years, trying to correct the damage done their son by his marriage to me. And I think their efforts are sweet. They are, after all, trying to work within the system.

When my copy of *Guideposts* comes, I usually drop my copy of Henry Miller or James Joyce's letters to Nora Barnacle or the paperback edition of *Truly Tasteless Jokes* and sit down for some inspiration. I like *Guideposts*, honest I do. I always read it straight through, being extra careful to skip the jock success stories. I feel about athletes the way I feel about cats and dogs: I'm glad they're happy, but I don't want to read about them.

My favorite *Guideposts* stories are usually about family crises: a mother-daughter failure in communication; a husband's infidelity (just like in the Old Testament, *Guideposts* thinks only husbands can be unfaithful: wives are always promiscuous); an alcoholic parent; a general and painful cooling of spiritual fires in one or more members of the family.

But crises occur outside the family as well: planes are about to crash over the Atlantic Ocean on a dark, stormy night; a senile old man is firing gunshots at the neighborhood children

---

*Reprinted by permission of the author.

who creep into his yard and pelt him with rotten eggs; a famous actor is tempted to Tinseltown but comes to his senses and develops a new spirit of humility.

The stories in *Guideposts* are all as dependably the same as chocolate pudding without lumps. Of course, I always rather liked a few lumps in my chocolate pudding, but I can see the value of smoothness. I've decided there is probably one *Guideposts* writing machine up there in Pawling, N.Y., and it is really turning them out. The machine may even be a person, for all I know. But all *Guideposts* articles have the same style, the same vocabulary range, the same rising curve of suspense, the same unraveling. Even the "Fragile Moments" columns are miniature versions of their big-moment parent stories.

Each story has a nice summary at the top, just in case you want a preview of upcoming events or perhaps plan to skip the story and go watch Clint Eastwood on HBO. I, for one, can't skip them. Here's one that says "Back in the not-too-long ago, there were people called 'hippies.' Other people did not always understand them." Well, I certainly would want to read that story, just to find out what position *Guideposts* is going to take with regard to the status of old hippies. Other eye-catching summaries are as follows: "How would you react if you read your own death notice?" "There are times when a bad fall can be a good thing" and "A group of businessmen under pressure to accept a thirty-day prayer challenge." I can't wait to fix me a glass of chocolate milk and sit down to read these stories.

Some of my friends poke fun at *Guideposts*, the worst mockers being Yale-type seminary graduates. My answer to them is if you think you're so great, why don't you put together a nice little magazine for secular humanists, agnostics and just plain superficial Christians? My minister friends don't know what to say to this challenge. They walk off muttering about simplistic solutions to the problem of faith in our times. Where they are going is to the porno place so they can empathize a little.

My favorite *Guideposts* stories can bring me to tears. I've got a Jewish friend who used to be married to a Catholic and is now toying with becoming a member of the Ethical Culture church: she cries, too. Sometimes, just to be mean, I hand her a *Guideposts* story and force her to read it so I can watch her mascara streak.

Anyway, I generally am very careful about when I read my *Guideposts*. The emotional effect is cumulative. I wouldn't want to be interrupted. I have sat in the wingback chair in my living room on a drab Tuesday afternoon when it's too late to nap and too early to drink and been carried right out of myself. *Guideposts* always gives me a sense of the urgency and significance of life.

When the old woman is fighting her way to the kitchen door through the smoke and licking flames started by a tipped-over kerosene lamp, I go with her. We cross that hot linoleum together, gasping for breath, feeling for sure that all is lost and we will never see our sixteen grandchildren and forty-two great-grandchildren again. But then, just when we are about to pass out for a lack of oxygen and the searing heat, we feel a peaceful, cool confidence enter us. We know, somehow, that we are not alone in this misery and that we will live if we will only be still and have faith. At this point, I have usually started nodding and crying. The old woman and I see, all of a sudden, a wet towel on the counter just above our heads. We had been using it before the fire started to mop up some spilled milk. We momentarily pause to reflect that spilling the milk is not always so terrible; then we grab the towel. Holding the towel to our faces and rubbing its cool wetness over our arms, we make our way slowly and purposefully to the kitchen door. Just as we fall, exhausted, into the back-yard, into the black, wet earth, an ambulance and fire truck pull up and we are lifted lovingly onto a clean white stretcher, to be taken to the hospital.

Stories like this one can give me renewed energy to stir the stew, speak softly to my children, reach out and touch somebody dear to me. I cannot resist a good, true ending. I know very well that everything that happens in *Guideposts* really did happen. I am glad that millions of people will be learning about life's miracles.

We could do worse than be readers of *Guideposts*. In fact, I'll bet there are no non-readers of *Guideposts* in foxholes. When you're down, what you need is up.

15

Freedom of religion. What does it mean? Among other things, religious freedom involves the right for any of us to act as stupidly as we please in religious matters. Hal Crowther questions some of the side effects of the current exercise of our religious freedom. The freedom granted by the Constitution is maligned, in Crowther's view, by an uncritical exercise of religious attachment to flawed, fallen, and utterly fleshly objects such as Elvis.

"HARMONIC CONVERGENCE— UFO CONTACTS & ELVIS AS A STATE RELIGION"*

by Hal Crowther

L ast year [1987] the "harmonic convergence" of the Mayan astronomers coincided with the 10th anniversary of the death of Elvis Presley, producing a tidal wave of cosmic energy and righteousness that killed Rudolf Hess and goosed the Dow Jones over 2700. There was a rumor that Ronald Reagan stirred in his sleep.

"There are people here that talk about Elvis like they talk about Christ," marveled one of the less devout of the more than 50,000 pilgrims who packed the city of Memphis to pray to the King who had fallen. All night the faithful kept a vigil by his tomb, in a bizarre parody of the myth of Easter. On mountaintops in Japan and California, on an island above Niagara Falls, the spiritual seekers waited for the same sunrise and tuned themselves for the celestial surge, or at least a few bars of "Blue Suede Shoes." But when the sun had

---

119

set on the day of reckoning and the stardust cleared away, Elvis was still dead and God was still playing possum. I don't mean to sneer. There's such a thing, I believe, as an energy field where a lot of minds pulling in the same direction create a force that's more than the sum of its parts. It was hard to get through the '60s without believing that. I'm not sure that a circle of spiritually charged individuals can levitate a table, say, but I suspect that they can rearrange its molecules, stir them up a little. This in spite of my own psychic shortcomings, my inability to merge with the surge. I missed Woodstock but I sat in on a few gatherings of the tie-dyed devout. On a hillside in Maine, in the rain, I once squatted squinting into the downpour with my ponytail dripping and listened to a few dozen of The People reaching out to the Oneness, imploring Him, I think, to stop the '60s from ending, though it was 1971. I was tremendously impressed by this tribal sacrament but not, as I recall, much possessed by it. Mantras sounded and nothing moved except the rain and my left hand, which kept reaching for the beer in my cooler though my companion kept shoving it away.

There was something real there. Which may be more than you can say for this harmonic convergence, based on calculations offered by an art historian in Colorado and denounced by most scholars and astronomers as flawed and bogus beyond salvage. None of the astronomical events predicted in Jose Arguelles's *The Mayan Factor* came close to occurring, in part because Arguelles misread his sources and got his dates wrong.

That didn't stop the mountaintop mystics from congregating by the thousands, and more than a published inventory of Elvis Presley's astonishing personal pharmacy kept his disciples from declaring him god-in-the-flesh (flash?). The blue-collar beauty of the Elvis cult is that its deity was so pathetically flawed. A high-testosterone singing voice notwithstanding, it was only the sexual power of that fatlipped sneer (remember in the '50s when magazines would try to inflame both sexes by showing his lips side-by-side with

Brigitte Bardot's?) that saved Elvis from earning his living as a forklift operator. No one had any reason to feel inferior to poor Elvis. The Graceland pilgrims may not look like much, but they've got themselves a god their own size.

About the right size, and the right spiritual hat-size, for the voodoo republic that's rising from the ashes of the one that Hamilton and Jefferson intended. By 2012, when the final cycle of Arguelles's bogus calculations ends in Judgment Day or in peace, love and UFO contacts, Elvis may be the state religion, and the crosses on our steeples may be replaced with guitars.

The timing is right. A voodoo republic is characterized by belligerent nationalism, bizarre allegiances and cults of personality, the proliferation of fatuous beliefs and a general disrespect for knowledge and for reason. Religion, politics and entertainment are joined together in a trivial trinity you can bring into focus by imagining Ronald Reagan in greasepaint, Elvis sneering on a candlelit icon and Pat Robertson kissing babies on the street. Drugs are epidemic and public taste turns to weird spectacles and simulated violence. Popular music is inane or incoherent. Journalism is predominantly lurid.

If you notice any of these symptoms, be sure and call me. Foreigners who think of themselves as friends of the United States report ugly new traits emerging. Shocked by the American crowd's partisan hostility as he humbled our Davis Cup team, West Germany's Boris Becker put the ball back in our court with something on it. He said he's never seen such nasty tennis crowds in any of the South American countries where the U. S. team has made crowd abuse one of its alibis for losing. The mood that Becker sensed spilled over into outright provocation at the Pan-American "friendship" games in Indianapolis, where morons in the crowd deliberately infuriated Cuban athletes by destroying a Cuban flag.

That isn't the country they explained to me in seventh-grade civics. Not a country where Oliver North, a rogue soldier with a nose twice the length of Pinocchio's, could flash his medals the way a coy stripper flashes her double-Ds and watch half the population coo and genuflect. Or where the *National Enquirer*, which becomes America's *Izvestia* when Elvis becomes its religion, could report that its readers support this saucy North (if "Little Egypt" is taken, can we call him "Little Iran"?) 15-1 for President of the United States.

The voodoo republic is characterized by a general suspension of skepticism, almost as if by martial law. When a disoriented population hungers for direction and commitment without subjecting their sources to any scrutiny, cults spring up around dead junkies, living rodents like Jim Bakker and almost any Oriental who can cull 20 ringing platitudes from the teaching of Kahlil Gibran. Not to mention certifiable megalomaniacs who talk to God and senile movie actors who talk to no one. The most mindless theology wins the most converts and indefensible nonsense like creationism parades in public as blood kin to science.

There is, I'm afraid, a connection and even a continuity between the peace-loving free spirits who bit on "harmonic convergence" and the apparent androids of the '80s who bite on fundamentalist voodoo and its poisonous political byproducts. Many of the children of the '60s took rationalism for a cold corporate plot, and purged it from their minds with ineffable notions and expansive chemicals. But once you've installed an effective filter on your brain, it will serve any purpose you turn to. I have reliable reports of ex-acidheads and flower-cultists who now embrace rightwing politics yoked to charismatic Christianity and even speaking in tongues. When your leap of faith becomes a broad jump, it can land you anywhere at all.

"America is the only country that passed from barbarism to decadence without ever experiencing civilization," sneers one European intellectual. English democracy without the deadweight of England's monarchy and its caste system was a magnificent experiment and probably the crowning achievement of the Enlightenment, but Jefferson's brainchild has descended into voodoo as a result of at least two errors I can isolate. One is the failure of public education, a noble and critical experiment that seemed to stop dead in its tracks when TV became a universal technology.

If you have any doubts about TV's lethal effect on the quality of literacy and public discourse in this country, read Neil Postman's polemic *Amusing Ourselves to Death*. History is its strong suit. Postman describes an 18th-century America with such a passion for ideas and the printed word that Thomas Paine's pamphlet *Common Sense* could sell in the neighborhood of 400,000 copies to a national population of three million, equal to gross sales of 24 million today. ("The poorest laborer upon the shore of the Delaware thinks himself entitled to deliver his sentiment in matters of religion or politics . . ." wrote Jacob Duche in 1772. "Such is the prevailing taste for books of every kind, that almost every man is a reader.")

It's easier to understand Thomas Jefferson's optimism about extending the vote. Nearly a century later (1854), as Postman describes it, an audience of country people in Peoria, Illinois, sat rapt through seven hours of oratory by Abraham Lincoln and Stephen A. Douglas, who spoke in a lofty idiom no longer considered suitable even in the college classroom.

Notions of progress are difficult to defend in 1987. Our other great error, I think, was a misreading of the principle of freedom of religion. The American colonists, many of them victims of religious persecution in England, wanted to make sure that no one in this country would ever be abused or ostracized on account of his faith. But at some point this was twisted to mean that religion was free from all legitimate scrutiny, free from fair comment, free from ridicule, from *laughter*. This excessive courtesy has encouraged voodoo mongers who are shamelessly self-righteous about beliefs that would, as Philip Roth's Portnoy observed, "shame a gorilla." Strange people should be free to worship Skye terriers as long as no one is harmed by it; but they harm everyone in the worst way when they apply the pressures that castrate the textbooks that make a farce of public education. The government can't be in the business of grading doctrine the way they grade meat: sensible; traditional but a question of faith, not for public debate; dubious; preposterous; tainted and dangerous. They can't, but I'd be happy to, as a public service. Or call any reputable divinity school.

As things stand now, the stage is set for Elvis to rise from his tomb and walk to the drugstore through clouds of light. When "Love Me Tender" replaces "The Star-Spangled Banner," don't ask me to sing along. I'll be Crying in the Chapel.

16

Aristotle said, "A man is known by his friends." It may surprise you, but even I, an ordinary pastor, have had the privilege of knowing some famous persons. Here is my tribute to two of them. Take these pieces as testimonial to my belief that the funniest of all God's creations are ourselves.

These first appeared in my column, "The Last Word," in the Christian Ministry.

"PARTNERS IN MINISTRY?"*

William H. Willimon

Would the person who introduced me to Pat Robertson please identify yourself? Without you, I would never have met the man, never have known a real-live presidential candidate, never have received monthly mailings and evening telephone calls asking for money. My relationship with Pat began in 1986 when I received a packet of tapes and pamphlets proclaiming that I had just joined Pat's "700 Club." The accompanying letter, personally signed by Pat, explained that my generous support was enabling "The 700 Club" TV program to reach millions of people every day. I also was helping to keep open a telephone line so that thousands of prayer requests could get through (4 million people called last year); to clothe and to feed millions of people through Operation Blessing; to sustain the CBN University; and to help "restore a biblical consensus to America." I would have felt great about that except that I had not given a dime to Pat. Someone else deserves the credit. Would you who sent in my name please identify yourself?

I really felt guilty when I received a gold 700 Club pin, a membership card, a copy of the Christian Broadcasting Network (CBN) *Partnership Newsletter,* two cassette tapes on Pat's four principles of success, as well as my first monthly giving card telling me that my gift would be used in accordance with Ezra 7:17-18. In checking the passage I see that Pat plans to use my generous contribution to purchase "bulls, rams and lambs." Don't they have livestock ordinances in Virginia Beach? No wonder "The 700 Club" reaches millions—you can smell it all the way to Washington, D.C.! If Pat is able to reach millions through the use of bulls, rams, and lambs, that's fine. But Ezra 7:18 troubled me because it tells Pat: "Whatever seems good to you and your brethren to do with the rest of the silver and gold, you may do. . . . "

I wrote and told Pat that I would love to take the credit for keeping his university afloat, the telephone lines open, Operation Blessing blessing, a biblical consensus restored, and bulls, rams, and lambs off the street, but someone else had given the money in my name. If he would be kind enough to tell me who it was, I would like to *pray* for that person.

In answer to my letter I received my December giving card asking for $15 or more to share the gift of eternal life.

One month's CBN newsletter informed me that Pat had designated his son Tim to be CBN's new president. I wrote Pat and asked why we members didn't get a chance to vote on Tim. In response, Pat sent my monthly giving card for March asking for a sacrificial contribution to support his work. I felt better about Tim after I read in the newsletter how the Lord had once led him to give $1,000 to CBN just before his wedding, money he had been saving for his honeymoon. The next day, a man offered to send Tim and his new bride anywhere in the world. They honeymooned in Greece. How would I have learned all that without knowing Pat?

Where do I find the person who enrolled me in the 700 Club and gave my name to someone named Gladys in Virginia Beach, who has been asking me for money? When I received my first personal correspondence from Pat, I thought not of rams and bulls in Ezra 7, but of the farmer whom Jesus describes in Matthew 13:24-30. Upon learning of the anonymous "gift" of some weeds amidst his grain, the farmer observed, "An enemy has done this."

To the person who gave my name to Pat, whoever you are, wherever you are, know this: With a friend like you, I don't need enemies.

"I WAS VANNA'S PASTOR"*

The other day as I was standing in the supermarket checkout line, madly perusing the latest *Star* magazine in an attempt to finish the article, "Vanna Says Nude Photo Is Cheap Shot" before I arrived at the cash register, the woman behind me bumped me with her cart and said, "Either move up in line, buddy, or let me by."

I turned and said to her in an indignant tone, "Madam, I'll have you know that you are addressing Vanna White's former pastor." She shrieked, and then asked me for my autograph. Everything came to a halt in the supermarket as people crowded around me. Before it was all over, the manager had given me a free copy of *Star*—after I promised always to shop at his store.

Although the *Star* doesn't report it, and you probably will not read about it in her new, long-awaited and hot autobiography, *Vanna Speaks*, it is true: I was Vanna White's pastor. The glamorous but taciturn beauty who turns letters on "Wheel of Fortune" was a leader in my church's youth group in North Myrtle Beach, North Carolina.

I admit that I can't detect the influence of my preaching when I watch Vanna turn her letters on "Wheel of Fortune." About the most they let Vanna say about theology is "Big

Money! Big Money!" But I am sure that it is there, however subtly.

I expect that her autobiography will contain no mention of my ministerial influence. When David Letterman asked Vanna about the most interesting men she has met, she mentioned only Merv Griffin and Tom Selleck. Perhaps she has forgotten my powerful sermons or the fascinating short-term course on "Christian Sex, Dating and Marriage" I gave the youth every year.

Perhaps.

But perhaps Vanna never speaks about her former pastor because she remembers the advice I gave her. One Sunday in May of her senior year at North Myrtle Beach High, I asked, "Vanna, what are you planning after graduation?"

She replied, in her unfailingly sweet and sincere way, that she had always dreamed of going into modeling, so she was going to modeling school in Atlanta.

"Vanna, no!" I said. (I flunked nondirective counseling in seminary.) "Don't do that! Those schools will do nothing but take your money. Nobody ever gets a job at one of those places. You have brains! Ability! You could be more than a model!"

She thanked me politely and said, "But I have this dream of going to Hollywood and becoming an actress."

"From North Myrtle Beach?" I asked. "Vanna, that only happens in movies. This is crazy!"

According to the *Star*, Vanna makes more in one week of taping "Wheel of Fortune" than I make in a whole year of giving good advice to aspiring teenagers.

17

Jewish comedian and writer Woody Allen has, throughout his illustrious career, enjoyed the fun and the challenge of growing up Jewish. In this sketch, Allen retells a classic biblical episode. "No sense of humor," mutters the well-modulated voice of the Lord to an utterly befuddled Abraham. And well might the Lord say the same to us children of Abraham.

"THE SACRIFICE OF ISAAC"*

Woody Allen

. . . And Abraham awoke in the middle of the night and said to his only son, Isaac, "I have had a dream where the voice of the Lord sayeth that I must sacrifice my only son, so put your pants on." And Isaac trembled and said, "So what did you say? I mean when He brought this whole thing up?"

"What am I going to say?" Abraham said. "I'm standing there at two A.M. in my underwear with the Creator of the Universe. Should I argue?"

"Well, did he say why he wants me sacrificed?" Isaac asked his father.

But Abraham said, "The faithful do not question. Now let's go because I have a heavy day tomorrow."

And Sarah who heard Abraham's plan grew vexed and said, "How doth thou know it was the Lord and not, say, thy friend who loveth practical jokes, for the Lord hateth practical jokes and whosoever shall pull one shall be delivered into the hands of his enemies whether they can pay the delivery charge or

*"The Sacrifice of Isaac," excerpt from "The Scrolls," from *Without Feathers* by Woody Allen, copyright © 1974.

not." And Abraham answered, "Because I know it was the Lord. It was a deep, resonant voice, well-modulated, and nobody in the desert can get a rumble in it like that."

And Sarah said, "And thou art willing to carry out this senseless act?" But Abraham told her, "Frankly, yes, for to question the Lord's word is one of the worst things a person can do, particularly with the economy in the state it's in."

And so he took Isaac to a certain place and prepared to sacrifice him but at the last minute the Lord stayed Abraham's hand and said, "How could thou doest such a thing?"

And Abraham said, "But thou said—"

"Never mind what I said," the Lord spake. "Doth thou listen to every crazy idea that comes thy way?" And Abraham grew ashamed. "Er—not really . . . no."

"I jokingly suggest thou sacrifice Isaac and thou immediately runs out to do it."

And Abraham fell to his knees. "See, I never know when you're kidding."

And the Lord thundered, "No sense of humor. I can't believe it."

"But doth this not prove I love thee, that I was willing to donate mine only son on thy whim?"

And the Lord said, "It proves that some men will follow any order no matter how asinine as long as it comes from a resonant, well-modulated voice."

And with that, the Lord bid Abraham get some rest and check with him tomorrow.

18

If God kept a diary, what would God say about us? Colin Morris, British Methodist preacher and head of religious broadcasting for the BBC, produced God's Diary. *He says, "I provoked a sizable correspondence from shocked believers who thought me irreverent and my talks blasphemous. . . . I am unrepentant. It was not presumptuous on my part to imagine I was privy to God's innermost thoughts. . . . I succeeded only in demarcating the infinite distance between the God who is the product of our . . . feverish imaginings and the One who is . . . above all things but not beyond their reach."*

"A WEEK IN THE LIFE OF GOD"*

Colin Morris

Sunday
These long-winded preachers! They mean well, but I fear their hearers will think I am a very dull deity. What is it about me that evokes such tediousness from some of the righteous?

Monday
I wish insurance companies would stop describing it as an act of God whenever there are floods and natural disasters! That is a very dismal view of my nature. Apparently I only intervene in human affairs when clever people can find no other rational explanation of things that happen to them. They must make up their minds. Either I am in all events or none. If I took special action every time millions of people asked for a favour the world would be in chaos.

*Reprinted with permission of Epworth Press.

The world as a whole depends absolutely on me. But when my children see my hand in some special event, they are saying something very important about themselves rather than me. They are saying that they saw my general will and purpose made plain to them in that event like a glimpse of the sun through a break in the clouds. Or else, like a flash of lightning on a clear day.

Tuesday

Here is a hard customer. He prays, 'O God, if you do not help me, I'll ask my rich uncle in America!' Faced with the threat of the almighty dollar, what can I do?

Wednesday

They have converted a disused church into a bingo hall. The new owners say bingo is a harmless social pleasure. They could not imagine God being unhappy about his now empty house being used to offer company and a little excitement to lonely people. I don't want to be a heavenly wet blanket but I cannot be complacent about the worship of blind chance. That strikes at my very nature. One of my names could almost be anti-chance. I am the essence of what is purposive rather than random in the universe.

Thursday

The church council have dismissed their minister after only six months because of his eccentric habits and his peculiar opinions. Well, he always was a bit of a fool but I've put up with his foolishness for sixty years yet these godly folk couldn't cope with it for six months!

Friday

He engaged in anguished inner debate. When ought he to make his peace with me? Well, I can help him there. I don't want to restrict his freedom so let's say he ought to make his peace with me one minute before he dies. Of course, he cannot know when he will die. So he'd better do it now.

Saturday
The philosophers are arguing about my existence again. I have news for them. My bare existence is the least interesting thing about me. Bare existence is boring—ask any cabbage or log of wood. To occupy oneself with arguments about my existence is like sailing the seas to discover an unknown continent, catching sight of it and turning back for home. 'What was it like?' their friends ask. 'No idea,' the explorers reply, 'But it's there all right.'

I have much more interesting things to do than merely exist.

And what can these scholars mean when they talk about my inaccessability? I am, they claim, elusive. Well, if they can't find me, the reason is simple. They can't find me for the same reason a burglar can't find a policeman.

Sunday
The faithful few gather in the old church with its peeling paint and rumbling boiler. They try hard to be hopeful as they struggle to keep the doors open and make an impact on their neighborhood. They should not despair. Those worshippers are dignified beyond their comprehension. They represent the wholeness of my church. If it does not exist in them, it does not exist at all. If the one, universal, holy church is not to be found in that dismal building, it is not to be found anywhere.

Monday
That Yorkshire farmer reminds me of the old Hebrews in his intense sense of place. As he left Matins this morning he bowed his head and said, 'Farewell, Lord, we're emigrating to Australia'.

Tuesday
I can understand the outrage of devout believers at the blasphemies sprinkled throughout modern conversation. But they shouldn't be too upset on my account. Even blasphemy

is a back-handed testimony to my existence. I have heard any number of 'God dammits!' and 'Christ almightys!' today but not a single 'Baal dammit!' or 'Woden almighty!' Only a live god gets cursed.

Wednesday

What I choose to give, no one can withhold—so those who rob humanity of my gifts do not long prevail. On the other hand, what I choose to withhold, no one can give—so those who play god are soon revealed as frauds.

Thursday

It is announced in Hollywood that an actor called Mr. Charlton Heston is to play me in a new biblical epic. According to the press release, among his qualifications are his craggy good looks, the fact that he has been married to the same wife for many years and that he is President of the Screen Actors Guild.

I can quite see why they chose him. But some of my best servants wouldn't have such qualifications. Paul was an ugly little man, Abraham was a polygamist and Martin Luther wanted to behead peasants who banded together to form unions. Of course, they were only human whereas I . . .

But Hollywood does make it hard for me to live up to their expectations. I recall Mr. Cecil B. deMille rewriting whole passages of the book of Exodus in order to smooth off some of the rougher corners of my character. I wouldn't wish to upset him, but I did prefer the book to the movie.

Friday

I cannot always give them what they ask for, not because they ask for too much but because they ask for what I do not possess. They cannot have square circles nor wet dryness nor curved straight lines. Nor can they have love without cost, life without pain, truth without effort. I cannot give them what I do not possess.

Saturday

Here's a man who claims he's on this earth by accident and that this accident is just one of an infinite series of accidents going back to the dawn of creation. Just fancy, he's the product of so many accidents! What a terrible insurance risk he must be. I'll bet he didn't get a Christmas card from the Prudential.

Sunday

I'm not too keen on that hymn they're singing—'Jerusalem, my happy home'. It purports to describe the delights of heaven in such terms as:

> Thy turrets and thy pinnacles
> With precious gems do shine,
> Thy very streets are paved with gold
> Surpassing clear and fine.

> Thy gardens and thy gallant walks
> Continually are green
> There grow such sweet and pleasant flowers
> As nowhere else are seen . . .

And so on in the same vein. Christians are such know-alls! I intend heaven to be a lovely surprise for them, but they are already anticipating it as a boring old extension of the Town & Country Planning Act.

Monday

Too many people play games with the Devil, like arm-wrestlers testing their strength. They should leave well alone. It is dangerous, even for playful motives, to contend against one who has nothing to lose.

Tuesday

I rejoice in the creative power of human beings, but it ought to be tinged with modesty. It has its proper limits. They have yet to create a new primary colour or a third sex or another dimension. I permit them to rearrange the basic elements of creation but not to add to them.

Wednesday

Some people are fortunate in being naturally good, yet they are still capable of complaining that I show mercy on the wicked. They ought to be grateful the scales of heavenly justice are exquisitely balanced. I have already shown mercy on them in creating them naturally good.

Indeed the good ought never to despise the wicked. Some reprobates please me for the reasons the conventionally virtuous could never fathom.

Thursday

Rumour has it that when I banished Lucifer from heaven he was asked what he missed most and he replied, 'The sound of the trumpets in the morning.' It is a fanfare of a different sort that heralds the morning for me.

The nuns troop into chapel for the morning office before it is light. Sister Fortunata shivers in the chill air and she moves very slowly because she is old and cannot see very well. As she lowers herself painfully on to her knees to pray, her arthritic joints crack. That for me is one of the important sounds of the morning—a Te Deum more precious than any words of the liturgy.

Friday

This poor woman is in torment. Again and again she tries to address me and dries up sobbing bitterly because she has lost the power to pray. It matters not. So long as she can weep, I am not much bothered about whether she can pray.

Saturday

A party of American scholars has just returned from Turkey where they claim to have found the remains of Noah's ark on

Mount Ararat. According to their measurements, they estimate the ark to have been 173 metres long, 29.7 metres wide and must have weighed over 3 million kilogrammes. I don't understand those measurements. If I had intended the world to go metric would I have chosen twelve apostles?

19

With joyful irreverence, novelist Beverly Coyle takes us to the Florida of the fifties where she grew up as the daughter of a liberal Methodist minister "who was not a strong pulpit man." Serving people in the little Florida towns along U.S. 1, her father exemplified for Coyle all those quiet servants of God who serve without fanfare in out-of-the-way corners of the Kingdom of God like Boynton Beach.

In this episode, a young girl watches her father baptize at, of all places, the beach.

"TAKING MARTHA WITH ME"*

From *The Kneeling Bus*

Beverly Coyle

My father was a Methodist minister, but since he was never a strong "pulpit man," he rose quite slowly in the hierarchy of Methodism. I grew up in large renovated parsonages all over rural Florida in the fifties. There were no religious pictures on the walls of those old furnished houses; my mother would not hear of it; my mother, Caroline, had been president of her sorority; my father was a liberal with advanced degrees who'd smoked cigarettes in the Navy. And I was taken to New York the summer I turned nine, where I saw Patty McCormack burn up her red shoes in "The Bad Seed."

So it was a shock for me to learn that spring when I was still nine that my father was going to immerse a woman named Mrs. Mollengarden in the Atlantic Ocean at the Easter Sunrise Service.

*"Taking Martha With Me" from *The Kneeling Bus* by Beverly Coyle. Copyright © 1990 by Beverly Coyle. Reprinted by permission of Houghton Mifflin Co.

My parents must have had reasonable conversations about it; how it actually came about that Mrs. Mollengarden had set her mind to a low-church ceremony; how Dad had already agreed to something so beyond his congregation's notion of good taste. Now they were breaking the news to my sister Jeanie and me, rehearsing their story for the larger fold.

"You're going to do it in the *ocean?*" Jeanie asked. Neither of us could quite grasp just how bad the situation was. There was still hope in the room for a simple sprinkling on dry ground.

But when my father didn't answer, we almost saw the whole thing and turned at once to look at Mother. Her lids fluttered bravely. "She has requested it," my mother explained. "Your father will take Mrs. Mollengarden out to the sandbar where the water is calm."

She might as well have said that he would take Mrs. Mollengarden out to the sandbar to be hanged by the neck until she was dead. We were better prepared to hand down that sentence to the woman ourselves than to be told that apparently all you had to do was ask for an immersion and it would be immediately granted to you.

I thought of Martha, the Baptist preacher's daughter, whom I tortured occasionally in the neglected mango grove that separated her family's parsonage from ours. Martha was something of a dirty yard girl with impetigo below the knees. She had the habit of pulling out her eyelashes, and from time to time I was observed bossing her around the properties. I knew my sister disapproved of even the simple convenience of this connection, and I feared her indictment of me now that we'd been told of Mrs. Mollengarden. And so I was surprised when, after an early supper, Jeanie invited me to leave the house with her. Jeanie could be counted on to sometimes love me in an emergency. We went to the town dump, where no children were supposed to go anymore since a man had exposed himself there to somebody in the high school.

My sister led me to a spot where she and her best friend, Celia, were planning to start a club. They had already cut windows in a refrigerator box and acquired orange crates. I knew I was never to come there again, but could sit inside for now if I was prepared to make fun of Mrs. Mollengarden, whom neither of us had ever met.

"She has big veins on one of her legs," I said. My kindlier self knew the woman was going to be merely doughy and hopeless, a woman without any make-up or good sense. But instead I invoked ugly details—crooked hips inside a sack dress, loose arms dangling down like monkey vine. Jeanie said none of it mattered; *she* wasn't going to the Easter Sunrise Service this year. No matter what.

I shifted my weight and thought about this challenge.

"I want to go," I admitted.

"So go," Jeanie said.

I looked at her. "I want to see how he'll do it."

"I'll show you how he'll do it, Carrie," and she grabbed me by my hair and pushed me under. I went down with a great gasp, screaming and laughing and kicking at the sides of the refrigerator box. " . . . in the name of the Father and the Son and John the Baptist," my sister said, "and when she comes up she'll be stinking . . . "

Jeanie didn't let go until she'd gotten in a terrific pull at the roots.

My father was out on the front lawn when I came up to report to him about Jeanie's clubhouse at the dump. He sighed and said we would all have to discuss this matter later, but for the moment did I want to come with him to Martha's house? He had asked Reverend Wenning if he could borrow a baptismal robe.

Of course I would come. I took up Dad's hand to lead him through the old mango grove. I was the only one in the family who had ever visited the Wennings on the other side, and besides the grove was full of hazards: old tires and tin cans and things I'd hauled in there myself. I made sure I led him over easy ground.

It was already twilight inside the big grove. The old trees had dropped blotched fruits of the day; mangos lay where they fell—split and exposed to flies. It was a freeze grove, and the still living trees were casting themselves away very slowly; they were dying in peace.

"Will you have her kneel down?" I asked. I steered him safely around the obstacles. He was making an effort to keep the deep, loose sand out of his shoes. I wouldn't have said anything in the world to hurt his feelings. I knew his family had been Assemblies of God, although it was not often mentioned, or them either. We had one photograph they'd taken of him in high-top shoes and a cotton dress with three starched flounces. He could have passed for some child on my mother's side, except that a detail in the picture gave everything away. There was no screen on the open window above my father's head.

"Dad! Will you have her kneel down?" I asked him softly.

"Who's that, sweetheart?" he said.

"Mrs. Mollengarden! When you get her out there will you have her kneel down or what?"

"Oh, I see what you mean," he said. "I suppose I could do that. To tell you the truth I haven't thought about it."

"You could take a pitcher out there with you," I said. "You could have her kneel down and then pour water on her head out of that pitcher." I already knew which of my mother's would be appropriate. A plain buff one with no stripes.

"Ummm," he said, "perhaps I could." And then we fell silent and I seemed to see the invisible path in front of us—the one I'd heard about, the one you traveled if you were a big enough person. It lay as the strait and narrow under my feet.

We marched formally up to the back screen door of the Wennings' rundown parsonage, where Martha was watching out for us. My father had telephoned ahead, and Martha held open the door to let us in. Reverend Wenning had the robe right there ready in the dark kitchen. It was a well-used, very plain maroon robe with lead sinkers sewn into the hem. He pointed these out to us in an offhand way while my father slipped the whole thing on. Mrs. Wenning murmured that it was a good fit, averting her eyes to the floor, where the robe fell in plumb lines above the tops of his shoes.

"I suppose I could fix up one of our choir robes this way," Dad said. I heard one of the sinkers crack again against his ankle bone.

Reverend Wenning was already saying it was no trouble to let Dad borrow this one. "You take it on with you, Preacher." he said. "This is an extra." Mrs. Wenning asked Martha to get a sack.

"Well, I appreciate it," Dad said. He made a point of taking the robe off as slowly as he could. Mrs. Wenning smiled and folded it carefully inside a brown bag from Winn Dixie. We shuffled politely out the screen door to discover darkness had fallen over their back yard. Martha went barefoot a few steps with us beyond the porch stoop, then paused to watch until we came to the edge of the grove.

"Good-bye," my father called out. I was not sure what I heard in his voice—the unfamiliar neighborliness of it all; Reverend Wenning having the robe there in his kitchen like that. "Thank you!" he called.

The next day was Saturday and I found her watching for me from Habakkuk—the largest tree in the grove. She had all the trees named for books of the Old Testament. From this tree we could see the small road that ran past our houses and the two churches that sat three blocks apart. Even in daylight the grove was shaded and cool. But the sun had dried the fallen fruit and dispersed the heavy odors.

As I climbed to a favorite limb I'd staked out for myself, I was pleased to hear that Martha was curious about the robe. "You don't have a baptismal pool in your church," she said, though it was not a boast. Martha was not a swaggerer. The previous summer she'd grown quite bruised and yellow from a case of what they called mango poisoning. She and her brothers turned bright orange before it was over and they'd all had to stay out of the grove for months. I wondered that she never thought to brag about this episode in our uneventful days—a girl who'd been poisoned and lived.

I lay back on my limb and stretched my arms over my head. I had schemes for almost dying like that—going to the brink and returning safely. It was to be like a push from a swing—the seat brought up impossibly high and hurled with a snap to send me face up into the blue.

"My dad won't *need* a baptismal pool, Martha," I said.

I could rarely count on her to keep to the subject, even when she tried, as she did now after a little pause. "Do you want me to take you over to look at the pool in our church again?" Martha asked.

"No, thank you," I said, knowing she well remembered how I'd tricked her into letting me see their baptismal pool back behind the pulpit; we'd discovered it enclosed with a heavy curtain she said they tied to one side whenever there was a need. The sunken square was as dry as a culvert and had bounced our whispers around until we'd scared ourselves. I regretted my earlier interest in this facility now that immersion had come so legitimately and effortlessly into my own life.

"Don't forget, I'm getting baptized this summer," Martha said.

"I know," I said.

"Are you going to come? Did you ask your mom yet?"

"Yes."

I heard her sigh in contentment.

"But I can only come if you invite me, Martha. You have to send me an invitation."

"Why?"

"So that way my mom will know it's all right with your mom."

"My mom don't care."

I sat up. "Well, she has to care, Martha. Your mom has to care. Don't be so stupid."

Now, Martha was thoroughly confused and she looked off somewhere else with those frightening eyes of hers. My mother had told her she had such lovely eyes that she ought not to do that, pulling out her lashes like that. To me it was another exotic accomplishment completely wasted on her.

"My mom wants you to come," she finally said.

"Then all you have to do is send me an invitation."

"All right," Martha said. Of course she wasn't sure what it meant to send an invitation, and I knew that perfectly well. I saw her wipe her eyes with the back of her hand.

"Oh, now don't tune up and cry," I said. I climbed down off my limb and sat beside her on hers. "I'll tell you a secret if you won't tell anybody."

"I won't," Martha promised.

"Do you know why my dad borrowed your daddy's robe?"

"No," Martha whispered. "He don't know either."

"Because my dad is going to immerse a lady . . . in the *ocean*."

And I was aware at that moment I had said sacred words—words that were miraculously joined with deed. I saw myself taking Martha by the hand and guiding her into the safety of my father's denomination, where she should be baptized any way she wanted now, where she would eat right and fill out, where her hair would thicken and her color would improve and she would go to college.

"What's the matter?" I said when I turned to find that she'd pulled back from me, as if of all times in her life she would choose this one in which to press her advantage. But it was a look of helpless dismay. Poor Martha was seeing bathing suits and inner tubes; she was smelling hot dogs and suntan oil.

"You mean," she whispered, "He's going to do it at the *beach*?"

Sunday was Palm Sunday, the immersion a week away, and upstairs in the parsonage I poured powder in my shoes and watched the street filling up with cars. We Methodists had an oyster shell parking lot behind the new educational plant. But the Baptists just pulled up anywhere. From the bathroom window I could see Reverend Wenning's congregation parking, on grassy littorals, pickup trucks and station wagons. They stood around talking with Bibles pressed against their chests, calling out encouragements to their children, who shouted back at them from the trees in the grove. As a rule I never saw Martha on Sundays, but I wanted to find her that morning to show her something, to set her straight about the matter of the beach. I slipped out the back door and sneaked up unobserved to my edge of the grove, where I could watch for her. I had never done this before and knew instantly that Martha never had either. The mango trees were full of boys.

In church that morning, we all stood at the end of the service and sang an Easter hymn. A very tall man behind me bellowed out over my head and into the reds in the windows, which shone bright cherry. "Up from the grave He arose, / With a mighty triumph o'er His foes." I counted all the straw purses strewn in the pews in front of me. Somewhere in the church was a straw purse that belonged to Mrs. Mollengarden. It would be decorated in shell flowers with bits of wire stem like all the other ladies' purses, but it suddenly came to me that she was a very large woman, and that when my father took her in his arms, lowering her down, learning over her, supporting her, raising her up again, surely,—for there was no other possibility—surely one of his arms, his *left* arm in fact, would touch Mrs. Mollengarden's front. I rehearsed it all in a large arena just inside my head. I stood hip-deep in early April waters and silently curved my father's man's arms around enormous spheres of space. There just wasn't a question in my mind but that his left arm was going to touch Mrs. Mollengarden's breast.

After church I told my mother in the kitchen that I thought he ought to have her kneel down.

"I hardly think that's necessary," Mom said, thrusting a set of napkins and silverware at me. She thought I was trying to dramatize the whole affair.

"But you see, if Mrs. Mollengarden would just kneel down," I began, but my mother simply turned away, repeating that she thought such a thing would not be at all necessary. She lowered her voice and whispered it. We children were not to worry.

And yet when the Sunday meal began, as we all sat and

watched Dad carve up a roast chicken, my mother reasoned aloud. The air would be cold next Sunday morning, she said, and after the immersion she wondered if he and Mrs. Mollengarden wouldn't need to jump immediately into the car and out of the wind, which would be coming up fast with the tide change. She'd been thinking how he'd need to have on something old and plenty warm under Reverend Wenning's robe. No one would see because it would be best if he simply arrived at the service wearing the robe.

Jeanie sat and stared at the chicken. Dad arranged the meat with some deliberation, as if he heard nothing. Every time he lifted a little slice and delivered it to its proper spot, the movement carried the easy suggestion that he was merely taking the bird apart and putting it back together again. My mother might as well have been speaking in tongues.

Well, there was no place to change except in the public bathhouse, she continued, and that was way up behind the dunes. No one would want to stand around waiting for him to change. If the air was unusually still there'd be sand flies.

"This looks delicious, doesn't it, girls?" my father said.

And we would have to remember to put towels in the car. None of us was to forget to remind her about the *towels*.

Had she let her imagination have full play, it would have probably involved that lovely Northern couple, Mr. and Mrs. Deaton, standing well dressed and dignified in the early morning light, watching Noel Willis, their favorite pastor, leading that large woman out to where Mom hoped the sandbar would be—not out so that nothing could be heard, but far enough to silhouette them demurely against the rising sun. Beyond that she could not go.

That afternoon I found my friend up in old Habakkuk.

"Get down," I said. "I want to show you something."

I waited with some impatience as she took special care to ease herself out of that tree, wipe her hands carefully on her print dress, then take from me the illustration I'd torn from one of my old Sunday school books. It showed John the

Baptist standing beside Jesus in what was without question the *Sea* of Galilee.

"There you are, Martha," I said.

Martha studied it a long time; she was immediately in love with the illustration, and I saw her bite her bottom lip as she silently named for herself all the principals.

"You see? Even Jesus was baptized in the ocean."

Martha nodded her head. It was the River Jordan, she said, though she continued to nod that she took my point to heart. I saw then she'd never been my adversary in this matter of the beach. She'd simply had a fleeting image of the place as she knew it in Florida—ice cream wrappers poking up in the sand and very loud Yankees.

I pointed out to her some of the details of the illustration which interested me: John the Baptist stood somewhat behind Jesus and had his hands folded in prayer. The dove, descending from heaven inside a sun ray, dominated the scene, and, if one looked closely, it did look more as though Jesus had simply had water poured on his head. He didn't look especially wet.

"That's the Holy Ghost," she said, pointing to the dove.

"The Holy Spirit," I corrected her softly.

"Yes," Martha said.

"You can keep this," I said.

She blinked at me. "I got lots of pictures, but I don't have this here one."

"You keep it," I said.

"And you can have it back whenever you get lonesome for it," she said.

We were quiet for some time before I spoke again.

"Martha, when you get baptized this summer, are you going to kneel down in the water or what?"

"Grown-ups kneel down," she said. "Children stand up."

"Why is that?" I said. I was starting to feel better already. Martha had a way of looking far off to a place where things were supremely uncomplicated.

"I could find out from my daddy," she said.

"No, that's okay," I said. "I was just wondering."

Then Martha sat right down in the sandy grove and put the picture in her lap. I walked around behind her and leaned myself against a trunk.

"It's real quick, isn't it?" I said.

"What?" Martha said.

"Getting baptized. It doesn't take long, does it?"

"No," Martha said, "but it lasts forever."

She pushed her fine blond hair out of her eyes and turned to look at me. "You don't remember it, do you?" she suddenly said. "You was just a baby, wasn't you?"

"That's right." I looked her straight in the eye. "I was christened by a bishop."

Martha's eyes widened.

"You don't have bishops, do you?" I said, offhand.

"No!" she said. "What was he *like?*"

"He looked nice," I said.

"Did they take any pictures of you?"

She could not have done a nicer thing than to ask to see photos. The Methodist ministers, posing in their creamy white suits, impressed Martha the most, I thought. Without my telling her, she saw that my christening had been an occasion. Those were district superintendents wearing the fashionable white suits of the day, and that was me in the white center, lying in the bishop's arms. I decided I could press her for more information while she studied the rest of the family album.

"And so when they kneel down, what happens then?"

Martha looked up. And I remember now how she must have looked, that Renaissance angels had no eyelashes. Michelangelo's Mary had no eyelashes. Martha could have been carved from pink marble. She got up slowly from the edge of my bed, knelt down on the floor, and crossed her arms over the front of her chest. Then she held her nose and leaned back as far as she could. Finally she pulled herself up and let her sweet breath out again. There was not a sound anywhere in the house. I could hear the waves flapping gently on the

148

shore, and, while I knew everything would be all right, I knew they wouldn't be the same either.

"Martha?" I suddenly asked. "Do you want to come with us?"

"Where?"

"Do you think your mom would mind if you came next week to our Easter Sunrise Service?"

Martha blinked and looked far off.

"I'll ask her," she said.

I don't remember the long week that followed. I do remember sleeping rather lightly the night before in my blue-papered room down the hall from Jeanie, who'd wangled a sleep-over at Celia's so she could ride out to the sunrise service with Celia's family. Unfortunately, after the service Celia's family assumed Jeanie would return to town with us and we assumed she would return with them. And so, twenty minutes after my father had tried to immerse Mrs. Mollengarden in the Atlantic Ocean—all of us piling into the car to get them out of the knifing cold—Jeanie was left stranded at Boynton Beach. And when the poor child was finally rescued, she was in hysterics because she'd had no dime and had been afraid to ask a stranger for one.

My mother blamed it on all our confusion and worry. Things had been so eventful. My father and Mrs. Mollengarden had actually stepped in a hole on their way out to the sandbar. For a moment there, with only a few seagulls scolding and dripping frantically over the water, there had been no sign of them. Then a few moments later they had both come up again a bit farther out, where their feet found the edge of the sandbar which we'd always taken for granted, little children paddling out to it six days of the week. When we saw the two grown-ups standing tall at last, the water out there only came a little above their knees. Dad and Mrs. Mollengarden appeared merely to be wading in the sunrise. And so finally the ceremony had begun. No one was able to hear a word he said because people were still stunned at the near drowning they'd just witnessed before he could get the deed done and lead the woman, quite shaken, back to shore; whereupon my mother gave up all decorum and rushed to meet them with bundles of towels, which fell in the water everywhere as Dad searched around his feet in the vain hope that his glasses might have washed up somehow at that very point.

I was the only one who was not mortified by the interminable flailing moments before they reached the sandbar safely, and so fortunately remembered forever and ever exactly the way he did it. His right arm went around her shoulders as I had imagined and his left arm swung gracefully and firmly over Mrs. Mollengarden's large bosom as he lowered her down and said the words and raised her up again while Martha and I stood waiting with the small congregation. We held hands the whole time and Martha talked softly but a great deal, which I had not expected of her.

"This is right before the dove comes down," she said first of all when the two of them stood face to face and prepared to make that lovely embrace. And while Mrs. Mollengarden was under, Martha said amen and nudged me so that I said it too, quite involuntarily. But when they stepped silently apart there on the sandbar, and when they waded cautiously back to shore in light that scorched the waters, Martha told me frankly that she'd seen the Holy Spirit out there with them and that the Holy Spirit had kept them aloft.

20

I close this expedition into religious humor with a sermon. "The Last Laugh" was preached in Duke Chapel by Dr. Clyde E. Fant, Dean of the Chapel at Stetson University, DeLand, Florida. Dr. Fant is one of America's great teachers of preaching, having written a number of books on homiletics. In this sermon, Dr. Fant takes a text from the first book of the Bible to say that, no matter how tragic or grim life becomes, the good news is that God will always have the last laugh.

"ON GETTING THE LAST LAUGH"*

A Sermon

Clyde E. Fant

Text: Genesis 17:15-21; 18:9-15; 21:1-7

There once was an old man who had a particularly difficult time staying awake in church. In those days a warden walked the aisles with a long hickory rod, tapping anyone on the shoulder who went to sleep. One Sunday when the old man nodded off as usual during the sermon, the warden sternly tapped him on the shoulder with the rod. The old man kept on sleeping. The pastor frowned, and the warden tapped the man on the other shoulder with the rod. He still went on sleeping. The pastor shook his head and frowned again at the warden, and the warden took the long hickory rod and hit the man on top of his head with it; whereupon the man fell out of the pew into the aisle, face down. He slowly opened one eye, squinted up at the warden, and said, "Hit me again, I can still hear him."

---

*Reprinted with permission of the author.

I doubt that the preacher got a laugh out of that, but the rest of us did. What makes something funny, anyway? A surprising amount of effort has been devoted to answering that question. Writers, comedians, philosophers, and even theologians—from Shakespeare to Cyrano (or Steve Martin), from Freud to Bergson, from Kierkegaard to Niebuhr—have tried to understand this very complex thing called laughter. And what do they tell us? Why do we laugh?

We laugh because something is ludicrous, surprising, unexpected, absurdly incongruous. For example, if you take a child to the circus and a clown walks in with a painted mouth and a bulbous nose and bizarre clothing, slips on a banana peel, and falls down on the floor, you're not going to laugh. It's funny to the child because it's completely incongruous to see an adult, a grown-up, dressed in funny clothes and doing silly things like falling down on the floor. You and I, on the other hand, get a laugh out of an old man down on his face in a church aisle delivering one-liners to a stuffy preacher.

Life has a way of bringing the absurd, the surprising, the incongruous to us. Sometimes we laugh, sometimes we cry; in our text Abraham laughed at God. After all, what would be more ludicrous, incongruous, or surprising than for a hundred-year-old man with a ninety-year-old wife to be told they were going to have a baby? Just when Abraham and Sarah had decided they would start sending out invitations to their golden wedding anniversary (or maybe their diamond wedding anniversary, who knows?) they were faced with sending out birth announcements.

Exactly what we need, Abraham thought. Sure. You promised us a child, God; you promised us that when we followed you, you unknown desert God, halfway around the world. But did we get it? No. And now we're old, and you know and we know that it's impossible. So now you're gonna make a little joke with old Abraham, huh? You're going to tell a hundred-year-old man with a ninety-year-old wife, "Congratulations; your baby is on the way!"

So Abraham fell on his face laughing (that's what the

Scripture says), and Sarah got the silly giggles behind the tent flap. And God said to Abraham, "What is she laughing at?" And Sarah said, "Hey, I'm not laughing," while she bit the side of her lip. And God said, "You are too!"

So God and Sarah got into a 'tis-'taint argument. But you can hardly blame God. It's no fun being laughed at. I still remember the first date I ever had in my life. It was almost the last date I ever had in my life. I was thirteen; the girl called me. She was a Catholic. She invited me to go to a Sodality dance. Now I was a Baptist; I knew precious little about dancing anyway, and I had no idea what a Sodality was. But I was invited to go to the old YWCA with her to a costume party dance. I asked, "What should I wear?" She said, "A costume; it's what a costume party is."

Well, it sounded like fun, so I tried to decide what I would wear. I thought everybody already had probably thought of wearing the Superman, Captain Marvel, and Dracula costumes—I was thirteen, right? I decided I would go dressed as Captain Midnight. Captain Midnight has long since passed into the realm of collectible comic books. But like most old heroes he wore a cape and a mask. I said to my mother, "How am I going to get a Captain Midnight costume?" She said, "We'll make one." I said, "Make one?" She said, "We can make one."

I said, "But it's a yellow cape." She said, "We can make one; it's no problem."

I said, "How?" And she said, "With crayons. We'll color it."

I said, "Mother—is this going to look all right?" She said, "Oh, yes! What you do is, you iron it. It makes the crayon permanent."

"Oh . . . I see."

So off I go, driven by my daddy, wearing black leotards, a yellow crayon cape, and a little black eye mask perched on my forehead. We pick up Sally Collette. She comes out in a gypsy costume, which except for a few bangles about the neck, looks about the way she dresses most of the time. I was a little disappointed, but I thought, "Well, a gypsy costume, that's a costume." Dad unloads us at the door; he says "I'll be back at ten when the dance is over." We walk into the room. I don't know a soul. All those kids went to St. John's; I didn't know any of them.

But that wasn't the worst of it. Not only did I not know anybody in the room, I was the only person in the room wearing a costume. One guy had on a sailor cap, and everybody else was wearing jeans and T-shirts. I've got on black leotards, a yellow cape; I'm thirteen.

I went and sat in an adjoining room on a horse-hair sofa beside one of those old lamps with a forty-watt bulb and fringe on the shade and ate vanilla wafers brought to me by a kind lady who also served me some little cups of red punch from time to time and asked me if I was sure I was all right. Wouldn't I like to come back into the dance?

After about an hour of that, I couldn't stand it anymore. I went outside and hid in the hedge. I stood next to the brick wall behind the hedge and watched the buses from the Trailways depot across the street come and go, until finally I took the only nickel I had in my leotards and went across to a phone booth, called my dad, and said, "Dad, if you love me, come get me."

If it hadn't been for the lime sherbet we ate on the way home, the whole evening would have been a total loss.

Laughter can be painful. Aristotle (that far back—I should have known) warned me; Aristotle said, "We generally laugh at deformities or defects." Quintillian said, "Laughter is generally in derision." Cicero said, "We laugh at the ugly and the strange."

The truth is, the one being laughed at is not the only one in pain. The sarcastic laughter of Abraham and Sarah at the door of their tent barely conceals their bitterness and their disappointment. They are cynical. They could not make the promise of their own lives come true, and they cannot believe God can do it either.

Great comedians, we're told, come from those peoples who suffer most. From the persecution of the Jews to the slavery of the blacks, pain has given birth to much laughter. Kierkegaard says that is because the comic is a way of escaping from despair, if only for a moment; that's why we human beings crave it so much. That's why Henri Bergson calls laughter a uniquely human thing.

Kierkegaard also says laughter is a prelude to faith. It is not faith, but it is a prelude to faith. Why? Because when we laugh we acknowledge our humanness, our limits. If we can laugh at ourselves we are saying, "I am not God; I do not run the world. I do not have the right to control your life, and I can celebrate your joys even as I acknowledge my limits."

Abraham had bet his life on a promise. God had promised Abraham, "I will give you a family, and that family will be a blessing not only to itself but to the whole earth." The promise had not come true. And then on that comic day God showed up at the tent with a great smile saying, "Abraham . . . now!" You see, God was showing them, and us, that God's promise is always born of the impossible. That which we cannot do, God can do.

From Noah's ark to the resurrection, God's promise was always born of grace, a gift out of the impossible: from Abraham's child, Isaac, to Hannah's child, Samuel, from Elizabeth's child, John, to Mary's child, Jesus, a promise was born out of the impossible. Paul, thinking about that grace, later said, "Now I understand why it was like that; it's so none of us could brag about ourselves and say, 'Look what we've accomplished!' but would have to say in humility before God, 'Look what God has given.'" So the message to us, as to Abraham and Sarah, is always the same: what we cannot do to fulfill the promise of our own lives, God can do.

So when the baby was born to the geriatric couple, God sure could have had the last laugh, but do you know what? He let them have it. And when Sarah laughs again it is the only time in the whole Bible when laughter is not sarcasm or derision, but pure joy. And she says, "Who could have believed this, that old Sarah should nurse a baby? Who would believe this, that my old husband could have a child? I know what we're going to name him, Isaac, Laughter." And it must have been more than average fun the first time she chucked the baby under the chin and little Laughter laughed.

What is the story for us, a long way from that ancient tale? The prophet Isaiah said: "Listen to me, all of you who are looking for escape, you who are seeking the Lord; look to the rock from which you were hewn, and to the quarry from which you were digged. Look to Abraham your father and to Sarah who bore you; for when he was just one person I called him, and I blessed him and made him many people. The Lord will comfort Zion; the Lord will comfort all her waste places, and will make her wilderness like Eden, her desert like the garden of the Lord; joy and gladness will be found in her, thanksgiving and the voice of song" (Isaiah 51:1-3).

"Let's see now what you're made of," our football coach used to say, "we're going to find out now what you're made of." And, like Israel we're made of the heritage of Abraham and Sarah, yes, but also that of a carpenter in a clown suit, dressed like a buffoon in a royal robe, with a thorn crown on his head and a dirty reed for a scepter in his hand, a peasant dressed like a king, a dying man on a cross with a sign over his head lampooning his life: King of the Jews. All of these, from Abraham to Jesus, believed God when life was barren and hopes were stillborn.

So remember this: the Kingdom still rides in on a donkey; the promise always comes forth from tombs. God can yet give birth to your dreams. The last laugh is God's—and yours.

Let us pray:

Oh God, we who are the most comic of your creation
Pause a moment to acknowledge our humanness.
Even in the face of our hard work and much learning
We confess that the miracle is not in our hands, but yours,
Giving to us the last laugh:
Not the first laugh of cynicism or despair,
But the last laugh of celebration and joy.
Through the clown on the cross.

Amen.